ROUTLEDGE LIBRARY EDITIONS:
18TH CENTURY PHILOSOPHY

Volume 8

AN INTRODUCTION TO KANT'S PHILOSOPHY

AN INTRODUCTION TO KANT'S PHILOSOPHY

NORMAN CLARK

LONDON AND NEW YORK

First published in 1925 by Methuen & Co. Ltd.

This edition first published in 2019
by Routledge
2 Park Square, Milton Park, Abingdon, Oxon OX14 4RN

and by Routledge
52 Vanderbilt Avenue, New York, NY 10017

Routledge is an imprint of the Taylor & Francis Group, an informa business

© 1925 Methuen & Co. Ltd.

All rights reserved. No part of this book may be reprinted or reproduced or utilised in any form or by any electronic, mechanical, or other means, now known or hereafter invented, including photocopying and recording, or in any information storage or retrieval system, without permission in writing from the publishers.

Trademark notice: Product or corporate names may be trademarks or registered trademarks, and are used only for identification and explanation without intent to infringe.

British Library Cataloguing in Publication Data
A catalogue record for this book is available from the British Library

ISBN: 978-0-367-13518-8 (Set)
ISBN: 978-0-429-02691-1 (Set) (ebk)
ISBN: 978-0-367-18459-9 (Volume 8) (hbk)
ISBN: 978-0-367-18462-9 (Volume 8) (pbk)
ISBN: 978-0-429-19643-0 (Volume 8) (ebk)

Publisher's Note
The publisher has gone to great lengths to ensure the quality of this reprint but points out that some imperfections in the original copies may be apparent.

Disclaimer
The publisher has made every effort to trace copyright holders and would welcome correspondence from those they have been unable to trace.

AN INTRODUCTION TO KANT'S PHILOSOPHY

BY

NORMAN CLARK

METHUEN & CO. LTD.
36 ESSEX STREET W.C.
LONDON

First Published in 1925

PRINTED IN GREAT BRITAIN

PREFACE

IT may seem strange that one perhaps more readily associated with the National Sporting Club than academic pursuits, should have written on Kantian philosophy; but I have studied Kant's works carefully for some years, and trust my book is sound so far as it goes. Its purpose (so far as it can be said to have any different from the many other works on Kant) is to provide an exposition of Kant's philosophy such as will bridge between the exhaustive commentary and the short sketch. I have endeavoured not only to cover Kant's works essential to his philosophy as a system, but also to illustrate generally his position in the history of thought, and the two rival " schools " in relation to which he developed his theory of knowledge. The book is divided into four parts. Of these, the first is mainly introductory : it traces roughly the development of Kant's thought in its relation to the Rationalism of Leibniz and Wolff, on the one hand, and the Empiricism of Hume, on the other, and also shows the ultimate issue he had reduced his problem to prior to writing "The Critique of Pure Reason." The next, and of course most important part, expounds the constitutive principles of knowledge

Kant taught in the Critique, or, in other words, shows how by his doctrine of the principles of a priori synthesis he confirmed the validity of the principles of science. And the third part (perhaps proportionately rather too full) deals with the Transcendental Dialectic, or Kant's Doctrine of Pure Ideas; expounding his theory of the nature of Reason, and showing how this faculty necessarily causes us to pass beyond experience and present to ourselves metaphysical problems. Kant's chief work thus covered, the remainder of the book is concerned with his ethical system as set out in "The Metaphysic of Morals" and "The Critique of Practical Reason," and concludes by tracing his philosophy up to its final theological position.

Of the works on Kant from which I have obtained assistance, the chief have been those of Caird and Kemp Smith—exhaustive commentaries almost too well known to need mentioning. I have used both of these very freely, in some instances adopting from them modes of presenting Kant's arguments; but I have rarely referred to them when so doing, holding as I do that this is not a wise practice unless one either quotes an author direct or is perfectly sure of accurately repeating the point he has made.

Whilst sincerely trusting I have not misrepresented Kant's meaning in any of my passages, I am only too conscious that, in the case of so subtle and profound a thinker, it is difficult to be emphatic on the point. I have, however, taken all the safeguards that lay in my power, having submitted the manuscript to several persons who have had a sound academic training in philosophy before handing it to the publishers and received from them confirmation of its soundness. Amongst these I should particularly mention my friend Mr. Stanley V. Keeling, John Stuart Mill, Fellow of Philosophy at University College, London, and Exhibitioner of Trinity College, Cambridge—a serious student of philosophy, who, though the last person to claim authority, took his fellowship with a thesis on Kant's work, and therefore appealed to me as qualified to express an opinion. Mr. Keeling very kindly worked carefully through my manuscript, and, after making several significant alterations, wrote, saying : " I have no hesitation in commending the work as a sound and interesting introduction such as will bridge between the exhaustive commentary and the short sketch. It seems to me a clear and accurate statement of Kant's chief doctrines, and readers who wish to gain a general knowledge of these before proceeding to more complete works should find it of considerable assistance."

I can only hope that others will be able to confirm Mr. Keeling's opinion, and accept the work for all it professes to be—an introduction designed to popularise Kant, and to bring still further readers to his works.

N. C.

CONTENTS

PART I

INTRODUCTORY

CHAPTER I

HISTORICAL ASPECT OF THE PROBLEM

Kant's generally recognised status in philosophy—His early education and later life—Through physics to metaphysics—Kant's broad achievements in philosophy—Subsequent philosophy mainly concerned with the extension of the two divergent paths his metaphysique left—The position of philosophy at the beginning of Kant's career—Rationalism *v.* empiricism—Failure of empiricism to explain the necessity involved in the principles of science—Ditto of rationalism to explain why observation and experiment were essential to scientific progress—The successful achievements of Galileo, Torricelli, and Newton in physics and astronomy involved two things ; namely, the necessity of observation and experiment to knowledge, and the successful application of mathematics to the concrete world—Kant sought for a theory of knowledge that would explain both factors—Kant first of the Leibniz-Wolff school, but later came under the influence of Hume—The latter's scepticism and its effect on Kant—Hume's explanation of the principle of causality and its inadequacy—Conclusions as to the general nature of Kant's problem—A foreshadowing of his solution of the same . . . . *Page* 1

CHAPTER II

PRECISE NATURE OF THE PROBLEM

General purpose of the chapter—*Criticism, Dogmatism,* and *Scepticism* in the Kantian sense—The distinction between pure and empirical knowledge—Necessity and universality as the criteria of knowledge a priori—Judgments and conceptions showing that the human mind is capable of knowledge a priori—Analytical and synthetical judgments—Synthetical judgments a priori—Synthetical judgments a priori as the fundamental principles of mathematics—Ditto as the fundamental principles of physics—The grand issue of the critical problem : How are synthetical judgments a priori possible ?—The transcendental method—*Dogmatical* philosophers—General nature of the task in hand   *Page* 27

PART II

THE CONSTITUTIVE PRINCIPLES OF KNOWLEDGE

CHAPTER I

TRANSCENDENTAL ÆSTHETIC

General nature and division of the critical enquiry—Kant's general conception of the relationship between sense and understanding—General problem of the transcendental æsthetic—Kant's distinction between the *matter* and the *form* of perception—Space and time as a priori forms of perception—Metaphysical exposition of space and time—Kant's proofs that space and time are a priori—Ditto that they are perceptions and not conceptions—Transcendental exposition of space and time—Kant's demonstration that the mathematical sciences are based on space and time perceptions—Ditto that they could not carry the necessity and universality they do unless such perceptions were a priori and not empirical—Conclusions of the æsthetic—Space and time are empirically real but transcendentally ideal—The distinction between the a priori space and time perception and such subjective determinations as colour, taste, etc., to which no ideality attaches   44

CONTENTS

CHAPTER II

GENERAL SURVEY OF THE ANALYTIC. THE DISCOVERY OF THE CATEGORIES

The general problem of the analytic and Kant's method of treating it—The relation of sense to understanding—General logic and Kant's transcendental logic—The three branches of transcendental logic corresponding to the parts of general logic dealing respectively with apprehension, judgment, and reasoning—The different divisions of the critique which these constitute—The part thought plays in perception generally, and roughly what Kant sets out to prove in this respect—The main divisions of the analytic and the purport of each—Kant's method of discovering the categories—The logical table of judgments as set out by Kant—The categories, or conceptions of objects in general, corresponding to these—Kant's classification and explanation of the same . . . . . *Page* 69

CHAPTER III

THE TRANSCENDENTAL DEDUCTION OF THE CATEGORIES

General purport of this part of the critique—What Kant means by a " transcendental deduction "—The general contention of the deduction—The transcendental unity of apperception and what this principle implies—The transcendental ego as distinguished from the empirical ego of psychology—The categories as the means of bringing the manifold of sense under the unity of apperception—But they cannot give knowledge except in relation to the sensuously given manifold—The union of understanding and sense—The categories by determining the inner sense of its form of time determine all perception, in that they fix the ways in which the manifold of sense is put together in time—The *synthesis intellectualis* and the *synthesis speciosa*—The categories as the conditions a priori of the possibility of experience are conditions a priori of the possibility of objects of experience—Examples showing that the conformity of objective synthesis to the unity of space and time is equivalent to its conformity to the categories—General conclusions of the deduction 94

CHAPTER IV

THE ANALYTIC OF PRINCIPLES

The general problem of schematising the categories—The translation of them into time—By determining the inner sense they thereby determine all sense—The schema as distinguished from an image—Number or time-series of schemata of the categories of quantity—Time-content or degree the schemata of the categories of quality—Time-order the schemata of the categories of relation—Time-complex the schemata of the categories of modality—These categorical time-determinations furnished the metaphysical principles of science—Kant's general division of the latter—General distinction between the mathematical and dynamical principles—The nature of the mathematical principles—The axiom of intuition—The anticipation of perception—The dynamical principles—Kant's final answer to Hume as presented in the three analogies of experience—The principle of the permanence of substance—The principle of causality—The principle of reciprocity—Kant's proofs of these—The postulates of empirical thought—The general conclusion with relation to the principle of the pure understanding—Science always assumes such principles—Kant's position in relation to Hume, on the one hand, and Wolff and Leibniz, on the other, as brought to completion in the analytic—Common misinterpretations of this position—Knowledge of things in themselves—The division of the world into noumena and phenomena—Knowledge of noumena in the positive and negative senses—The impossibility of the former but justification for the latter—Criticism of Kant's position in relation to noumena—His "refutation of idealism" apparently misconceived by critics—External experience at any rate as real as internal, if not more so—But both only knowable as phenomena . . . . *Page* 123

PART III

TRANSCENDENTAL DIALECTIC, OR THE DOCTRINE OF PURE IDEAS

CHAPTER I

THE IDEAS OF PURE REASON. RATIONAL PSYCHOLOGY AND ITS PARALOGISMS

How is metaphysics possible as a natural disposition of the mind?—General statement of Kant's treatment of the problem—Kant's theory of the nature of reason—The goal of reason is the unconditioned—What Kant means by a transcendental idea—The true syllogism and the dialectical syllogism—The difference between the unconditioned as idea, and the unconditioned as cognoscible object—The nature and origin of the three classes of transcendental ideas—The problems these ideas present—The three branches of the transcendental dialectic, and roughly how they arise—Kant's treatment of rational psychology—The general errors of the latter—The vicious circle involved in trying to know the ego by the categories—The confusion between the transcendental subject and the object of the inner sense—The four paralogisms of rational psychology—Kant's conclusion in relation to the problem . . . . *Page* 160

CHAPTER II

KANT'S CRITICISM OF RATIONAL COSMOLOGY. THE ANTINOMIES OF PURE REASON

General statement of Kant's treatment of the problem—How the four cosmological ideas arise—More precise definition of the origin of the same—The cosmology ideas as distinguished from rational cosmology—The impossibility of rational cosmology demonstrated by the antinomies its assertions necessarily involve—The nature and origin of these antinomies—Kant's proofs of the theses and antitheses of the same—Human interests on the side of the thesis—Ditto the antithesis —The same reason that supplies the antinomies must enable us to solve them—General statement of Kant's solution—More explicit solution of the mathematical antinomies—Ditto the dynamical antinomies—The cosmological ideas as regulative principles—Kant's critical reconciliation of freedom and necessity—The freedom of the will as decided on these grounds . . *Page* 179

CHAPTER III

THE IDEA OF GOD. KANT'S REFUTATION OF RATIONAL THEOLOGY

General statement of Kant's treatment of the problem—The nature and origin of the idea—The totality of possible experience taken as a thing in itself, hypostatised and personified—The general problem of rational theology—The three arguments of rational theology and why they all fall back on to the ontological argument—Kant's refutation of the physico-theological or teleological argument for the existence of God—Ditto the cosmological—Ditto the ontological—General conclusion in relation to the problem . . 212

CHAPTER IV

THE IDEAS AS REGULATIVE PRINCIPLES

The ideas of reason and their function in relation to experience—The ideas as the means of giving unity to the concepts of the understanding—Such unity only subjective and logical, not objective—The principle of homogeneity—Ditto specification—Ditto affinity or continuity—The same cannot be realised in experience, but are essential regulative principles—The use of the ideas as ideal objects giving unity to knowledge 236

PART IV

KANT'S ETHICAL SYSTEM

CHAPTER I

THE PROBLEM OF MORAL FREEDOM

The critiques of pure and practical reason, and the relation of their problems—The negative treatment of freedom in the first critique—Negative freedom made positive by the moral consciousness—The opposition between man's sensuous propensity and the law of reason . 248

CONTENTS

CHAPTER II

THE FORMULATION OF THE MORAL LAW

General relation of Kant's moral system to the history of ethics—The determination of a good will as the sole criterion of moral worth—The criterion of a good will best found in the idea of duty—Respect for the moral law alone constitutes the moral worth of an action—Moral action as reason acting on a motive derived from itself—The opposition between man's sensuous propensity and the law of reason as set out in the critique of practical reason—The three theorems by which Kant reaches his categorical imperative—The first formula of the moral law applied to the duties of perfect and imperfect obligation—Ditto the second formula—The third formula and the idea of a kingdom of ends—Moral feeling . . . . . . *Page* 261

CHAPTER III

KANT'S MORAL THEOLOGY

The summum bonum and the problems it raises—The Immortality of the soul as a necessary postulate of the same—Ditto the postulate of God—Kant's moral theology as compared with Christianity—The relation of the postulates to the three ideas of theoretic reason—Is knowledge of the latter extended thereby?—A knowledge of God from the practical standpoint—The adaptation of man's cognitive faculties to his ultimate destination 279

INDEX 297

AN INTRODUCTION TO KANT'S PHILOSOPHY

PART I

INTRODUCTORY

CHAPTER I

HISTORICAL ASPECT OF THE PROBLEM

REGARDED by many as the most encyclopædic thinker since Aristotle, Emmanuel Kant has the distinction of having introduced a great revolution into philosophy and yet stood the test of time in almost singular degree. Modern philosophers may agree or disagree with much of his work, but the fact remains that they are rarely able to philosophise profoundly without reference to it, and on one point they are all emphatic —that no philosopher of this or any other time is to be more strongly recommended to students seeking an insight into the true philosophical problems. By common consent he stands as one of the great foundation-stones of modern thought, remarkably alike in scope and originality ; and as an individual achievement in metaphysics his chief work, "The

Critique of Pure Reason," probably remains unsurpassed to this day.

The philosopher's life-story presents little of significance beyond the evolution of his thought. Born at Konigsberg in 1724, he was the son of a local saddler, but his grandfather (his name was spelt Cant) had emigrated from the North of Scotland towards the end of the seventeenth century. Kant's father, a man in very humble circumstances, was able to give his son little assistance; but, thanks mainly to Franz Albrecht Schultz, a pasteur and professor whom Frederic William maintained as a kind of dictator in all matters theological and educational in Konigsberg and East Prussia, he received a sound early education at the Collegium Fredericianum, then the principal school in the province. It is clear that he remained under Schultz's care until he was seventeen years of age, and that he afterwards attended the University of Konigsberg; but, on the latter part of his university career being cut short by the early death of his father, he seems or the next twenty years to have been compelled to earn a pecuniary living by acting as a tutor to the better class families in the Konigsberg district, albeit he still continued to read hard and at the age of thirty-one managed to return to the university and take his degree as a Doctor of Philosophy. Despite his privations, Kant evidently gained a big knowledge of both science and philosophy during this period of his life; for in addition to publishing a number of significant treatises on physical subjects, he grew profoundly engrossed in metaphysics and laid the foundation of much of the thought that later made him so famous. But recognition was very slow in coming to him, and it was not until he had reached the age of forty-six that he received his first and only official appointment—that of professor of logic and moral philosophy at his old university. To a man of Kant's spartan habits this appointment meant an easy economic independence, however, and for the remainder of his life he was able to devote the majority of his time to the construction of his philosophical system. Year in year out, he pursued his task with an almost unrivalled patience and persistence. Strange though it may sound in contrast to the revolutionary effect of his thought, it is a fact that never once in his life did he cross the border of his native province; and despite his being a frail, half invalid little man, his servant is said to have called him winter and summer at five o'clock in the morning and to have stated that for thirty years he never knew him fail to respond Kant's thought was of such a profound and comprehensive nature as to be necessarily of very slow growth. Far from being one of those thinkers who spring into early fame by one great thought only, he had many metaphysical discoveries to be systemised and tested; and, though in his early manhood he published several treatises of considerable importance, his serious philosophical writings did not begin until he was forty. Before his great work, "The Critique of Pure Reason," was published he had reached the age of fifty-seven, and it was not until the last twenty years of his life that his pen was most active in giving the critical philosophy its complete expression. His life, like his work, was a triumph of perfectly calculated method; never hasting, never resting, he pursued his task with an almost clock-like regularity; and when, at the age of nearly eighty, he became a worn-out, half imbecile old man, he had the satisfaction of having accomplished work that has been placed on a level with the French Revolution, so important a factor was it in determining the life and intellectual features of the nineteenth century.

As previously stated, Kant's early writings were nearly all on physical matters; indeed, he is said to have understood Newton as well as he did Leibniz and Wolff, and his "Natural History and Theory of the Heavens," written fifty years before Herschal and Laplace came into prominence, was itself a notable attempt to explain the origin of the solar system on Newtonian principles. But we are now only concerned with his philosophy. Here Kant's work was to introduce the third great epoch in the history of the World's philosophical thought. By his distinction between phenomena and noumena, between things as the human mind knows them and as they are in their unknowable selves, he introduced into philosophy what might be regarded as a Copernican revolution. He considered he had irrefutably shown that the forms of mind are not the result of nature, as many Empiricists had thought, but that mind prescribes its forms to nature, and that the laws of nature, and indeed the whole of nature as we know it, has no existence as such independent of mind. His general achievements in philosophy have been admirably summarised by Schopenhauer in a passage in his " World as Will and Ideas." " Kant " (he says) " showed that the laws which reign with inviolable necessity in existence, i.e. in experience generally, are not to be applied to deduce and explain existence itself ; that thus the validity of these laws is only relative, and that consequently they cannot be our guide when we come to the explanation of the existence of the world or of ourselves. All earlier Western philosophers had imagined that these laws, according to which phenomena are combined, were absolute laws conditioned by nothing ; that the world itself existed only in consequence of and in conformity with them ; and therefore that under their guidance the whole riddle of the world was capable of solution. Kant exhibited these laws, and therefore the whole world, as conditioned by the form of knowledge belonging to the subject ; from which it followed, that however far one carried investigation and reasoning under the guidance of these laws, yet in the principal matter, i.e. in knowledge of the nature of the world in itself and outside the idea, no step in advance was made, but one only moved like a squirrel in its wheel. Thus, all the dogmatists may be compared to persons who supposed that if they only went straight on long enough they would come to the end of the world ; but Kant then circumnavigated the world and showed that, because it is round, one cannot get out of it by horizontal movement, but that by perpendicular movement this is perhaps not impossible. Kant ventured to show by his teachings that all those dogmas which had been so often professedly proved were incapable of proof. Speculative theology, and the rational psychology connected with it, received from him their death-blow."

This was Kant's broad achievement, but the methods by which he worked out such conclusions cross the whole of philosophy ; and to those who wish to make a serious study of metaphysics his system is to be commended as probably the most central in the history of thought. Subsequent philosophy has been mainly concerned with extending the two divergent paths his metaphysique left. On the side of *form*, for instance, it has been extended by Hegel, Fitche and Schelling, and the present day absolute idealists ; on the side of *matter* by Herbart and Schopenhauer, Lotze and many others. But when the more dogmatic of these opposing extensions are eliminated, no one can be very emphatic on the advance alleged to have been made. Often, even during the last hundred years, the cry of " back to Kant " has arisen, and certainly, few philosophers have held the balance between speculative and empirical ideas with a stronger and steadier hand, or provided a theory of knowledge so capable of reconciling conflicting beliefs. By studying Kant's work one will, not only gain a profound insight into the problem of knowledge, but see clearly expounded the consistency of the facts of science and the fundamental religious dogmas; how, for instance, theological ideas like teleology and the freedom of the will may be quite compatible with the mechanism of nature; and how, finally, the moral consciousness may be sufficient to give a knowledge of the spiritual world, and with it a conception of God and His purposes.

Failure of both Rationalists and Empiricists to Account for Science

But before proceeding to the Kantian solutions of the philosophical problems, or even to his conception of what the problems resolved themselves into, it is necessary to take a view of the state philosophy had brought itself to at the beginning of Kant's career; for then, and then only, shall we understand the circumstances that led to Kant writing "The Critique of Pure Reason," the great work in which he sought to examine the nature of human knowledge and to determine its precise limits.

To start with, it appears clear that at this time philosophy was in a great state of what might be called creative confusion. With the Age of Enlightenment, as the eighteenth century was called, the dogmatism of the earlier philosophers of modern times had been forced to give place to Reason, and Reason, in its new-born enthusiasm, had thought itself capable of ultimately solving all problems; the only question was how. But later the spirit of criticism that had banished dogmatic tradition threatened to overthrow Reason also, and was seriously questioning Reason's capability of dealing with the philosophical problems no matter how it went to work. With the rise of David Hume and his scepticism, we find the absolute validity of all knowledge seriously disputed, and that not only with relation to questions transcending experience, which Hume dismissed as completely beyond our ken, but even with respect to matters concerning our world of experience, as, for instance, the objective truth of causal necessity, or the law of the uniformity of nature. Moreover, as a result of this doubt of reason's powers, there came an influx of mysticists and sentimentalists, only too anxious to support the contention that reason was a useless weapon because of their own lack of it, and all saying in effect: " the greatest truths are to be found in man's inner nature; if he is to attain to true philosophic knowledge, he must be guided by his general feeling," etc. etc.—contentions which, however true, must certainly mean the death of progressive philosophy.

Amongst the genuine philosophers, however, the real issue at stake was seen to resolve itself into the controversy between the two great schools of philosophy respecting the nature and validity of knowledge; it was a battle between the Empiricists, on the one hand, and the Rationalists, on the other.

To explain the theories of each in a few sentences is to be anything but accurate, for there were many different forms and degrees of both Empiricism and Rationalism; but for the sake of illustration it is perhaps sufficient to define the most extreme forms of each. With such latitude, then, the Empiricists may be regarded as those who contended that Knowledge was explicable from experience. Human beings simply had sense experience, recorded what they sensed, and in time started to think and judge in accordance with certain modes of association constantly found in experience. Very briefly, knowledge was sense transformed, and even the mind's mathematical ways of reasoning, its methods of thinking in terms of likeness and difference, cause and effect, substance and accidents were all deducible from experience, or at least, from experience and certain ways of associating it. With Hume and extreme Empiricism there was therefore no such thing as necessary and universal knowledge. Our minds had become what they were because we had had certain uniform sense experience; indeed, even our most complicated ideas and the principles of association they followed (resemblance, contiguity in time and place, and cause and effect) were all to be explained on similar empirical lines. It thus followed that had our sense experience been different, our methods of thinking would also have been quite different; and since experience for all we knew might change at any time, it was clear that the inferences of which all our ideas consisted could never yield absolute certainty but at the most only probability.

The Rationalists, on the other hand, saw that there was that in knowledge that could not be explained on these lines. Judgments in geometry, arithmetic, and in certain propositions in physics implied a logical necessity and universality that could never have come from experience. Far from being sense transformed, knowledge was only explicable from reason, the extreme Rationalists contended. It consisted of certain innate ideas, which exist in the mind a priori, independent of all experience, and sense, instead of assisting to truth, was greatly "confused thinking." This philosophy was thus concerned mainly with the logical necessity in experience; insisting, above all, on the great difference between mathematical propositions having an a priori source, and mere opinions based on experience and differing according to experience. All real knowledge, it was contended, was like mathematics; mathematics began with certain definitions, then, by an analytical process, a process of unravelling what was implicit in that already known, was able to go on extending its knowledge with absolute truth. It was believed that accurate knowledge of the world could only be arrived at by understanding the primary qualities of things, which were mathematical in their nature; the secondary qualities—smell, sound, colour, etc.—were regarded as unreal. These philosophers thus came to regard the world as mathematical in its nature; observation and experiment they thought of as of comparatively little purpose. Just as in mathematics one was able to take a definition and extend one's knowledge by working from it in accordance with certain a priori modes of reasoning, so in time science would be able to do the same of the material world. Starting from a few central truths, it would be able, by logical and mathematical reasoning, to reduce the world to a vast mechanical system, all the intricacies of which would unroll themselves with absolute necessity, causal relations resolving themselves into reason and consequent.

All is not clear from this, to be sure; from such a short definition of Rationalism it may appear that the Rationalists in contending that sense experience was only "confused thinking" were almost absurd. But for the purposes in hand it is sufficient merely to sketch the two theories of knowledge very roughly, and to show the inadequacy of both—the latter a task which the exponents of the two rival theories naturally did very fully in their perpetual controversies. Thus, the Rationalists contended that Empiricism gave no satisfactory explanation of the necessity contained in mathematical judgments and certain propositions in physics. If our ways of thinking had come from experience alone, all judgments being synthetical judgments a posteriori, as some Empiricists contended, then there was no reason why some judgments should carry necessity and universality, and others should be mere matters of opinion differing with individuals. But no one could fail to see a great difference between the two. "All men are mortal," for instance, was a judgment formed from experience, every man in the world's history so far having died, but no one could say that it carried necessity. Yet, such judgments as "two straight lines cannot enclose a space," "two and two make four," "every change has its cause," certainly did carry such mathematical and logical necessity; indeed, one could not even think otherwise. Accordingly, if these judgments came from experience, as the Empiricists contended, how was it that other judgments ("all men are mortal," "night follows day") exceptions. which were just as unknown in experience, should yet be so different? Clearly there was in knowledge an element of necessity that distinguished it from mere opinions based on experience, and this element Empiricism failed to explain.

On the other side, the Empiricists had plenty of opportunity to show the forthcomings of the Rationalist theories. If knowledge was explicable from reason alone, and simply consisted of analytically unravelling certain a priori ideas in accordance with the laws of thought (Identity, Contradiction, and Excluded middle), how was it that observation and experiment were always essential to scientific progress? Again, the Rationalists' view of the nature of space and time was very unsatisfactory. No one could deny that there was a great difference between the reasoning out of a geometrical proposition and the observing of how things were actually arranged

HISTORICAL ASPECT OF THE PROBLEM 13

in space and succeeded in time ; and, with Newton, who had become convinced that astronomy implied an absolute space, the Empiricists contended that space and time did not permit of the Rationalistic explaining away. They were elements that implied observation as the primary factor in knowledge, it was contended, and Descartes' idea that the world would in time be explained in the terms of pure mathematics was clearly a vain one.

Now the exponents of these metaphysical theories might have continued their opposition endlessly without getting much further, but, as is often the case with theory and practice, practice was going ahead and theory learnt much from trying to keep pace with it. In the seventeenth and eighteenth centuries physics and astronomy were making sure and steady progress, and as the nature of physical experience grew more explicit the metaphysical problem to be explained naturally grew more definite. Indeed, the experiments and successful achievements of Galileo, Torricelli, and Newton all directly concerned the main points of dispute amongst the Empiricists and Rationalists ; for both the discovering of the laws of motion and the advance made in astronomy involved the two things the opposing theories of Knowledge were respectively strongest and weakest in—first, the necessity of observation and experiment to knowledge, and secondly, the successful application of mathematics to the concrete world. Each side naturally claimed the evidence in favour of its theory of

Knowledge. The Empiricists pointed to the success of Galileo, and said : " This man instead of thinking out in the abstract how bodies *ought* to fall, takes bodies of different known weights and drops them from the top of the leaning tower of Pisa and *observes* how they *do* fall " ; and in like fashion, they referred to the combined achievement of Kepler and Newton in astronomy, saying : " Not only would such an achievement have been impossible without observation, but the achievement, coming as it has greatly as a result of observation, is sufficient to definitely confirm the reality of space." But in reply the Rationalists were able to say : " Yes ; but all these scientific achievements mean the successful application of mathematics to the physical world, and the necessary character of causal relation, and no theory of Knowledge that does not uphold these can possibly explain such achievements." Astronomy was pre-eminently a science which involved both observation and the apprehension of necessary relations ; and whilst both the Empiricist and Rationalist theory of Knowledge each respectively accounted for one of these factors, neither successfully accounted for both in conjunction. What was wanted was a theory of Knowledge that, whilst insisting on observation as one of the primary essentials to Knowledge, was also capable of explaining why the facts observed always fell under such necessary relationships as to make them scientific, and until Kant's coming no philosopher had successfully accomplished this.

KANT'S EARLY TRAINING AND THE SUBSEQUENT INFLUENCE OF HUME

Now it is essential to an understanding of the Kantian philosophy that one should know something of the metaphysical school he first came of, also of the subsequent influence the scepticism of Hume had on his thought; for a great deal of his work is not understandable except in its relationship to the modifying of these two extremes.

Kant was first of the Rationalist, or dogmatic school, as he afterwards called it. During the early part of his career he came greatly under the influence of Leibniz and Wolff, both of whom were great disciples of Descartes, and believed that both matters of experience and the problems transcending experience could alike be solved by a priori reasoning. Wolff's system of metaphysics held sway at most of the German Universities of the time. It began with a general doctrine of pure Being, or Ontology, and then broke up into three parts dealing with the special kinds of being—World or Cosmos, Soul, and God—and by pure reasoning he sought to determine the character of each of these. His Rational Cosmology was a doctrine of the nature of the World, his Rational Psychology a doctrine of the soul as permanent substance and spring of all conscious life, and his Rational Theology a doctrine of God or the Infinite Being. To his mind all these were capable of proof, and as we shall afterwards see, much of the Kantian criticism is devoted to these doctrines.

Kant, as stated, was considerably influenced by the Leibniz-Wolff philosophy in the earlier part of his career, but later he came across the work of the English Empiricists and the writings of Hume, and it was Hume who " awoke him from his dogmatic slumber," as he puts it, and ultimately led to his formulating the critical problem. An arch-empiricist, Hume drew the conclusions of the empirical theory of knowledge more logically and forcibly than any of his predecessors. If all knowledge was the outcome of experience alone, all ideas being nothing but copies of experiences, then knowledge of non-empirical existence was impossible : Rational Cosmology, Rational Psychology, and Rational Theology were completely beyond our ken. Indeed, even our knowledge of matters of fact, the propositions of physics, could carry no absolute necessity and universality ; probability was, strictly speaking, the most that could be attributed to such knowledge. We had no knowledge of necessary connection or of substance ; though it was true that ideas are not entirely loose or disconnected, one idea naturally leading to another, as, for instance, a picture leads to thoughts of its original, night to the idea of darkness, and pain to the thoughts of a wound, these connections (resemblance, contiguity, and cause and effect) were only a matter of association arising from habit or custom ; and when philosophers talked of an a priori and necessary

HISTORICAL ASPECT OF THE PROBLEM

connection between notions like cause and effect, substance and accidents, etc., they were giving mere habitual associations a logical necessity and universality which they do not in fact possess. Hume, in short, held that our ideas follow one another in a certain order simply because they are the outcome of certain uniform sense experience, impressions of one kind always being found associated with impressions of a certain other kind in the three ways mentioned; but we could not say that our ideas necessarily follow the order they do, or that the world of experience would continue to be true to such ideas. Strictly considered, our principles in physical calculations would not necessarily be found to always hold good of experience; for subjective habit could never be a perfect anticipation of objective fact. Though by supposition we attain a knowledge carrying much probability, this was the most we could say of knowledge of matters of fact; necessity and universality of the type philosophers had attributed to it was clearly out of the question.

Now Kant was greatly perturbed by Hume's scepticism, particularly with regard to its denial of the necessity in knowledge of matters of fact. Whilst he was not reluctant to deny the metaphysical theories of Leibniz and Wolff as far as matters transcending experience were concerned, he believed with the Rationalists that mathematics and certain propositions in physics carried necessity and universality, and from this period we find his whole philosophy concerned with criticising the dogmatism of the old metaphysicians, on the one side, and scepticism of Hume, on the other; and in reading the Critique it is very necessary that this dual task should always be kept in view. But though Hume's scepticism stirred Kant to reaction, it was Hume himself who, strangely enough, to a great extent gave Kant the key which enabled him to refute his theories. In considering the nature of our judgments about the world of concrete experience Hume had raised a profound problem. He had noticed that we never contemplate any effect without at once necessarily connecting it with its cause, and that the scientist in going to work takes the principle of causation, or the principle of the uniformity of nature, as it is now more often called, for an established fact when investigating nature. Yet, as Hume pointed out, all we really observe in contemplating nature is succession and change; actual cause, or any necessary connection between phenomena prior and subsequent to change, we never observe. It seems, therefore, as though we are so constituted that when we contemplate or reason about succession and change we give it subjectively a necessity and uniformity which in itself it does not possess. Whilst objectively, in experience, the phenomenon presented to us is nothing but succession and change, no sooner do we think about it than we regard it as bound together in terms of cause and effect, and feel that there is necessary logical connection between the two, a tie binding the cause to the effect. What is the explanation of it? As Kant was quick to see, Hume had here raised a profound problem, but the Scottish philosopher was too much convinced that all knowledge was empirical to satisfactorily explain it. As we have seen, Hume held that our ways of thinking were all to be entirely explained as the result of sense experience found to be associated in certain uniform ways, and the best explanation he could therefore give was that the necessary connection which the mind forms of changes in the external world is a habit our minds have formed from custom, due to continually seeing the same succession. We observe objects succeeding one another, and similar objects being constantly conjoined—heat following flame, snow following cold, the movement of one billiard ball following the movement of the other that knocks it, etc. etc.; then, having found that in many instances two kinds of objects have always been conjoined, we suppose that the objects are causally related, that the one is the cause of the other. In other words, Hume's contention was that, after repeated association of similar changes, we are led to expect the appearance of the one kind of object on the appearance of the other; by habit or custom the mind is carried to believe that the two objects in question are connected, that they will always go together, and hence that like causes always have like effects.

We shall deal with Hume's theory of causality more fully later when we come to explain the

Kantian metaphysical principles of science; for the time being it is enough to notice that Kant saw it to be a totally inadequate explanation. To Kant causal judgments, like mathematical judgments, carried necessity and universality; and Hume's explanation of causation failed to account for this. His theory gave no explanation of the power of anticipating principles so commonly believed to be necessary; it failed, moreover, to explain the difference between apprehension of succession and succession in apprehending, and really involved a denial of objective change. Yet, on the other hand, Hume's explanation certainly showed beyond doubt that the Rationalist theory of Knowledge was quite inadequate to explain causation; for though the Rationalists were right in their contention that we do not get the *principle* of causation from experience alone, Hume's criticism clearly showed that it was essential to go to experience for the discovery of causal laws. The Rationalists' contention that judgments of causation were analytical was obviously wrong; the mind does not discover causation by analysing a cause and finding it must by its very nature produce such an effect. However much the *principle* may be a priori, knowledge of causation is always dependent on observation, and in bringing this clearly to light Hume had shown the inadequacy of the Rationalist theory of Knowledge to account for physical science, even if he had equally failed to explain it on his own empirical grounds.

THE NATURE OF THE PROBLEM AND A FORESHADOWING OF KANT'S SOLUTION

Thus, Kant, after following closely the scientific progress made in his time, and pondering on the Rationalist and Empirical theories of Knowledge, sees that both are inadequate in their explanation of empirical science. From the progress of Galileo and Newton in physics and astronomy, it was clear that these sciences involved both observation of facts and apprehension of necessary relation—a combination neither Rationalism nor Empiricism could explain. And in like fashion, Hume's criticism of causation demonstrated the same thing; for though it showed the necessity to observe facts to gain a knowledge of causation, Hume had certainly failed to account for the principle by saying it had come from experience.

Further, not only were both Rationalism and Empiricism unable to account for science, but in their explanations of morality and religion they were little more successful. On the one hand, the Rationalists pointed out that, inasmuch as both morality and religion dealt more with what ought to be than with what is, any theory like Empiricism, contending as it did that everything in the mind comes from experience, could never explain a moral *ought*. On the other hand, as against Rationalism, the Empiricists had only to refer to the unnatural conclusions reached by Hobbes when he tried to explain morality and religion on the mechanical modes of reasoning advocated by Descartes to show that such work, resulting as it did in determinism, left no room for morality at all.

In the two greatest departments of human life—science and religion—current philosophy had failed, then, and Kant started with a clear consciousness of this double failure. From their sure and steady progress, and the necessity and universality involved in their principles, it was perfectly clear that mathematics and physics were genuine sciences; whereas metaphysics, far from showing the same progress, had throughout consisted of so many marches and counter-marches—one school of philosophers professing to have proved all the metaphysical dogmas, another school just as confidently asserting that, not only were metaphysical problems completely beyond our ken, but that even our knowledge of matters of fact carried no absolute necessity. Metaphysics had proceeded in this unsatisfactory fashion, Kant insisted, because (in spite of Locke's enquiry) it had proceeded without any real criticism of its powers. What was wanted was a complete examination of human reason such as would investigate the possibility or impossibility of necessary and universal knowledge, its sources and boundaries. Mathematics and physics were obvious sciences; if we could only find out how the mind is constituted to make them possible, we should then be able to test for ever the pretentions of metaphysics. And to this end Kant wrote "The Critique of Pure Reason"—the great work in which he not only tests for ever

HISTORICAL ASPECT OF THE PROBLEM

the mind's powers of solving metaphysical problems on rational grounds, but gives a theory of knowledge that satisfactorily explains the nature of science and reconciles the conflicting theories of the Empiricists and Rationalists.

Without giving the reader more preparation, it is of little use going into the contents of this work, but it may be of interest in concluding the chapter to show roughly how Kant solved the problem we have discussed. He agrees with the Rationalists that the human mind is capable of necessary and universal knowledge, in mathematics and physics, and that such necessity and universality cannot be accounted for by experience alone. But though this element in knowledge cannot have come from experience, but must depend on the very nature of mind itself (being a priori to all experience), the Empiricists were right in saying that without experience there could be no knowledge. To knowledge two main factors are necessary—experience (i.e. sensation) and certain pure forms of mind (i.e. a priori modes of sensibility and apprehending). In so far as the Empiricists insisted on the first factor they were right; in so far as the Rationalists had contended that the mind's ways of knowing could not be explained from experience, they too were right. To Kant there are two kinds of factors present in knowledge. Firstly, that which is given through sense—the a posteriori factor; and secondly, the pure forms of sensibility and understanding, which are not derived from experience but exist a priori in the mind as necessary conditions of sensibility and understanding, and without which experience would be impossible. In other words, Kant's theory is a distinction between the *matter* and *form* of knowledge. The matter of knowledge is the data of sense. These data of sense are then taken up into or perceived under pure forms. The forms of sensibility are space and time; by which is meant that my mode of sensibility is so constituted that in order to be conscious of the sensations I get I have necessarily to place them in space and time; space and time are pure intuitive forms of sensibility. This is the first step in knowledge. Next, the sense perception, which has come about as the result of the conjunction of the matter and the pure forms of sensibility, comes under a process of conceptual knowing, i.e., is brought under certain conditions of knowing common to all human minds— the a priori pure modes of thinking, which alone make experience possible and which provide the judgments carrying necessity and universality.

All knowledge is therefore knowledge of phenomena only, i.e., knowledge of things as the mind is compelled to make them appear in order to know them at all, and far from the mind having been formed from nature, as the empiricists had thought, mind prescribes its forms to nature, i.e., makes the data of sense fall under certain laws. Thus, in a certain sense the laws of nature are known a priori by the very nature of mind itself. Our data of sense might be quite different from what it now is, but the laws of nature, the mind's necessary mode of perceiving, connecting and relating its sensuous impressions, would still remain the same, because our modes of sensibility and thought are such as to make them fall under certain uniform laws.

As far as the two main considerations Kant had in view, then—the limiting of the scepticism of Hume, on the one hand, and the contentions of Leibniz and Wolff that knowledge could pass beyond experience, on the other—the situation is clear. We have necessary and universal knowledge of the principles of experience, and Hume was wrong in denying this; but in his denial of the contentions of Leibniz and Wolff that knowledge could pass beyond experience, Hume was right; for, however necessary and universal the forms of knowing, sense data are always essential to knowledge, and of the supersensuous we can have no knowledge at all. Otherwise expressed, our a priori forms of knowing are such as to make the data of sense fall under certain universal laws of experience, but these a priori forms have no use or meaning except in relation to the data of sense, and when metaphysicians like Leibniz and Wolff use these forms in relation to the supersensuous they are simply carrying on a process of unification without any subject matter to unify. It is therefore clear that on purely logical grounds we can have no knowledge of God, the real nature of the world, the freedom of the will, or the immortality of the soul. Though, as problems, such ideas are real in the sense that reason by its very nature presents them to itself, logical answers to them entirely transcend the scope of the human mind; indeed, if it were not for our moral consciousness, or practical reason, as Kant calls it, they would necessarily remain quite insoluble.

So much for the results of the Critique of Pure Reason in rough. It has been sufficient here to show the historical nature of the problem, the conflicting streams of thought which Kant was criticising, and to foreshadow the way in which he reconciled them. The process by which he came to such conclusions, his methods of dealing with the various philosophical problems, will be the work of later chapters.

CHAPTER II

PRECISE NATURE OF THE PROBLEM

IN the last chapter we traced the historical aspect of the problem Kant had to meet, showing particularly how the advance of science, the inadequacy of both Rationalism and Empiricism to account for this, and Hume's criticism of causation, led him to formulate the general Critical problem. We now turn to the more exact nature of the issue. In the " Prolegomena " Kant sets this out in three questions :—(1) How is pure mathematics possible ? (2) How is pure science of Nature possible? and 3) How is metaphysics possible ?—if not as a science, at least as a natural disposition of the mind. We shall endeavour to show exactly how these questions related to each other, how and why the answers to each depended on the same fundamental basis, and how ultimately the whole issue resolved itself into one question, for the solution of which Kant was led to formulate a new science—the science of the principles of synthesis a priori, with which alone the Critique of Pure Reason is really concerned.

But before dealing with the Critical philosophy it is necessary to understand what Kant means by

Criticism as opposed to what he calls *Dogmatism*, on the one hand, and *Scepticism*, on the other. In the popular sense Dogmatism is usually taken to mean the procedure of one who holds a conviction without reasons, but this, of course, is not what Kant means, for that would obviously be no philosophy at all. The philosophic Dogmatism to which he refers is the attempt to philosophise without first of all examining the instrument with which the philosopher does so, or to use his own words, it "is the positive or dogmatic procedure of reason without previous criticism of its own faculty." For Kant this is one extreme in philosophical method—any philosopher who takes such conceptions as cause and effect, substance and accidents, as giving definite knowledge without first considering their nature is for him dogmatical; the other is *Scepticism*, and by Scepticism he means the despair of all knowledge, born of the experience that "whatever is asserted can with equal truth be denied", and hence a belief that ultimate truth can never be attained. The philosopher of the latter type usually feels himself less biassed and broader minded than the Dogmatist, but, as Kant points out, in a certain sense Scepticism is equally a form of Dogmatism; hence what Kant insisted was that, if philosophers were to get any further, they would first have to employ some method over and above both Dogmatism and Scepticism, in that it was critical of the presuppositions that these two methods either use or reject without having first properly examined them. The only way to do this was to try and reach the fundamental principles of thought which both parties (and for that matter all other human minds) must alike employ in order to argue or be conscious at all ; and it is to this procedure that Kant gave the name of *Criticism*, since, to use his own words, it is " a criticism of the very faculty of knowledge itself."

Now on first consideration it may be objected that such a procedure is impossible, since in criticising the faculty of knowledge we should only be applying mind to mind, and consequently our knowledge would still remain object for a subject ; and certainly, if we go about the enquiry as Locke did in his " Essay on Human Understanding ", this objection would be unanswerable, for such an enquiry would be entirely phenomenal and we should still be in the domain of psychology. But, as we shall see more clearly later, by *Criticism* Kant does not mean an enquiry of this kind : his method is not psychological, but epistemological or transcendental. He means an enquiry into the nature of mind so far as mind is presupposed in the knowing of anything, or, in other words, an examination of mind so far as it is possible to find in it principles through which everything else must be known and without which nothing can be known. *Criticism*, in a word, is an examination of the preconditions of our having any knowledge at all.

From this it will be understood why Kant opens " The Critique of Pure Reason " by saying that what is wanted is "a science which shall determine the possibility, principles, and the extent of human knowledge a priori" (prior to all experience). To simply carry on as philosophers have in the past, those on the one side building up elaborate proofs of God, Freedom, and Immortality, without first ascertaining whether it is within the powers of mind to do so, and those on the other side contradicting them without having made any closer examination themselves, was simply to act dogmatically. Before we try to solve philosophical problems we must test the powers of pure reason (of reason independent of experience, that is to say), making a careful examination of what extent (if any) the human mind is capable of knowledge a priori, the exact nature of such knowledge, and finally, how far (if at all) it is capable of dealing with problems transcending experience.

Thus, the first thing the Critique has to do is to distinguish between empirical knowledge and knowledge a priori; for, although Kant is convinced that all our knowledge must begin with experience, as he states, it by no means follows that all arises out of experience. On the contrary, "it is quite possible that our empirical knowledge is a compound of that which we receive through impressions, and that which the faculty of cognition supplies from itself (sensuous impressions giving merely the occasion), an addition which we cannot distinguish from the original element given by sense till long practice has made us attentive to and skilful in separating it." The question, therefore, is whether there exists a knowledge, or at least preconditions of knowledge, altogether independent of all sensuous impressions—knowledge a priori, by which term Kant does not mean what the term is popularly taken to imply, i.e. knowledge independent of this or that kind of experience, but knowledge independent of any experience. Opposed to this is knowledge a posteriori, or knowledge through experience, and to divide these two sides Kant calls the one *pure* knowledge, the other *empirical* knowledge.

The first problem thus presented, then, is this: presuming we do possess pure knowledge a priori, how are we to distinguish it from the empirical, a posteriori, element with which it becomes compounded? What criterion is there by which we may distinguish a pure from an empirical cognition? Kant replies that a certain way of distinguishing the two is the test of necessity and universality. If a proposition contains these elements, it is a judgment a priori; for all empirical judgments, however far they may exhibit assumed and comparative universality (by induction), can never carry necessity and strict universality. Of all empirical judgments the most we can ever say is that, so far as we have hitherto observed, there is no exception to this or that rule; but, on the other hand, in the case of a priori judgments, there is such necessity and strict universality that we cannot even think otherwise. We may take a few examples to make this clearer. To take first some empirical judgments, "all men are mortal", or "all bodies are heavy", are statements which no one has ever experienced any exception to, yet no one would say they carry necessity and strict universality; the most we can grant them is assumed and comparative universality. But, on the other hand, if I say "every change has a cause", or "two straight lines cannot enclose a space", I am expressing a judgment implying, not merely a comparative universality which has so far always been found to apply, and which I think will in all probability always apply, but a necessity and strict universality such as admits of absolutely no exception, and which indicates a peculiar source of knowledge, namely a faculty of cognition a priori. Necessity and universality are, therefore, infallible tests, says Kant, for distinguishing pure from empirical knowledge, and are inseparably connected with each other.

Now, as suggested by the two examples above, it is clear that in knowledge we have judgments which are necessary and in the strictest sense universal, consequently pure a priori. Mathematics and physics provide plenty of examples. Indeed, according to Kant, if we take the proposition given above, "every effect has its cause", we see the conception of a cause so plainly involves the conception of a necessity of connexion with an effect, and of a strict universality of the law, that the very notion of a cause would entirely disappear were we to derive the conception, as Hume thought, solely from experience. Besides, as Kant points out, we might easily show such principles to be a priori by showing they are the indispensable basis of the possibility of experience itself; for if all the rules on which our experience depends were themselves empirical and consequently fortuitous, our experience itself could not acquire certainty. Moreover, not only certain judgment, but even certain conceptions are of an a priori nature. "If we take away by degrees from our conception of a body," says Kant, "all that can be referred to mere sensuous experience—colour, hardness or softness, weight, even impenetrability—the body will then vanish; but the space which it occupied still remains, and this is utterly impossible to annihilate in thought. Again, if we take away, in like manner, from our empirical conception of any object, corporeal or incorporeal, all properties which mere experience has taught us to connect with it, still we cannot think away those through which we cogitate it as substance, or adhering to substance, although our conception of substance is more determined than that of an object. Compelled, therefore, by that necessity with which the conception of substance forces itself upon us, we must confess that it has its seat in our faculty of cognition a priori."

Thus, we conclude that necessity and universality are not only infallible criteria of knowledge a priori, but that in the sphere of human cognition we possess such knowledge both in certain judgments and conceptions.

Analytical and Synthetical Judgments
Synthetical Judgments a priori as the Principles of all Pure Sciences

Having pointed out that the human mind is in possession of a priori knowledge, Kant, before proceeding to the question of its exact nature and how many forms it takes, makes a most acute examination of the exact nature of human judgments—an examination that, as far as synthetical judgments a priori are concerned, must be regarded as epoch making in philosophy and one of the most satisfactory explanations of the necessity in knowledge ever put forward. There are two main classes of judgments, he states, analytical and synthetical, and the difference between them lies in the two different ways the subject is related to the predicate. Either the predicate B belongs to the subject A as something which is already contained in it, and only needs to be elucidated (in which case the judgment is analytical); or else the predicate B lies completely out of the conception A, and adds something to the conception (in which case the judgment is synthetical). In the first case the connection between the predicate and the subject is cogitated through necessary logical laws of thought (of Identity, Contradiction, and Excluded Middle, or generally, of consistency); in the second, it is not cogitated in this fashion at all, but is a genuine extension which no amount of analysing of the subject could bring about. When, for example, I say, " all bodies are extended ", I express an analytical judgment, for the very conception of body implies extension. But if I say " all bodies are heavy ", the predicate is something totally different from the mere conception of a body ; it goes beyond the subject and extends it, and the judgment is therefore synthetical.

Now all analytical judgments obviously carry necessity, and of these we need say nothing more ; but on the other hand, synthetical judgments present a most significant problem to philosophy, and it is here that Kant's work was so entirely original. It is perfectly clear to start with, that all empirical judgments are synthetical ; for if, for instance, I say, " some men are mortal ", I can only gain the predicate " are mortal " from experience and no amount of analysing of the conception " *man* " will tell me this without going to experience ; and it is thus evident that it is experience that the synthesis of the judgment rests on. But what Kant very significantly points out is that there are some synthetical judgments that do not rest on experience alone, and the problem presents itself : Whence does the synthesis arise ? He takes as an example the proposition, " everything that happens has a cause ", and points out that such a judgment cannot be analytical, for the conception of a *cause* can never arise from analysing *that which happens ;* nor, on the other hand, can it arise from experience, for experience can never give the necessity and strict universality that the judgment carries. Whence, then, does the synthesis arise? In Kant's own words: "How am I able to assert concerning the general conception—'that which happens'—something entirely different from that conception, and to recognise the conception of cause although not contained in it, yet as belonging to it, and even necessarily? what is here the unknown—X, upon which the understanding rests when it believes it has found, out of a conception A a foreign predicate B, which it nevertheless considers to be connected with it? It cannot be experience, because the principle adduced annexes the two representations, cause and effect, to the representation existence, not only with universality, which experience cannot give, but also with the expression of necessity, therefore completely a priori and from pure conceptions."

From this example and others given by Kant it thus becomes clear that the human mind is in possession of synthetical judgments a priori, and having got thus far, Kant proceeds to show that these judgments form the principles of all pure sciences. He starts with mathematics, and here we have one of his greatest philosophical discoveries. Prior to Kant's time, it was held that as mathematical conclusions all proceed according to the principle of contradiction, the fundamental principles of the science were also to be recognised and admitted in the same way. But the notion is fallacious, says Kant, for " although a synthetical proposition can certainly be discerned by means of the principle of contradiction, this is possible only when another synthetical proposition precedes, from which the latter is deduced, but never of itself." Since, then, mathematical propositions are not analytical, and yet carry necessity, so cannot have come from experience, we have no alternative but to decide that they are synthetical propositions a priori. Kant's own words should be given in the explanation of this difficult question. "We might," he says, "at first suppose that the proposition $7+5=12$ is a merely analytical proposition, following (according to the principle of contradiction) from the conception of a sum of seven and five. But if we regard it more narrowly, we find that our conception of the sum of seven and five contains nothing more than the uniting of both sums into one, whereby it cannot at all be cogitated what this single number is which embraces both. The conception of twelve is by no means obtained by merely cogitating the union of seven and five; and we may analyze our conception of such a possible sum—(7 and 5)—as long as we will, still we shall never discover in it the notion of twelve. We must go beyond these conceptions and have recourse to an intuition which corresponds to one of the two—our five fingers, for example, or like Segner in his 'Arithmetic', five points, and so by degrees, add the units contained in the five given in the intuition, to the conception of seven. For I first take the number 7, and, for the conception of 5 calling in the aid of the fingers of my hand as objects of intuition, I add the units, which I before took together to make up the number 5, gradually now by means of the material image of my hand, to the number 7, and by this process, I at length see the number 12 arise. That 7 should be added to 5, I have certainly cogitated in my conception of a sum $=7+5$, but not that this sum was equal to 12. Arithmetical propositions are therefore always synthetical, of which we may become more clearly convinced by trying large numbers. For it will thus become quite evident that, turn and twist our conceptions as we may, it is impossible, without having recourse to intuition, to arrive at the sum total or product by means of the mere analysis of our conceptions. Just as little is any principle of pure geometry analytical. ' A straight line between two points is the shortest,' is a synthetical proposition. For my conception of *straight* contains no notion of *quantity*, but is merely *qualitative*. The conception of the shortest is therefore wholly an addition, and by no analysis can it be extracted from our conception of a straight line. Intuition must therefore here lend its aid, by means of which and thus only, our synthesis is possible."

So much for mathematics ; but not only arithmetic and geometry, but in like manner physics, contain synthetical judgments a priori as fundamental principles. This will be clear if we examine two of its leading propositions : viz., " in all changes of the material world, the quantity of matter remains unchanged " ; and that, " in all communications of

PRECISE NATURE OF THE PROBLEM

motion, action, and reaction must always be equal ". For in both these it is clear, says Kant, that not only is necessity contained and that they must therefore be a priori, but that they are synthetical propositions. No amount of analysing of the conception of matter will show me that it is permanent ; in the conception of matter I merely cogitate its presence in space, and to add to this its permanency I need to go beyond what is contained in it, and this I do not empirically but a priori. The proposition, like all the others of pure physics, is therefore a synthetical proposition a priori.

The Grand Problem of the Issue

From the above it is clear, then, that both pure mathematical science and pure science of nature have synthetical propositions a priori as their fundamental principles, and that it is this that distinguishes them from mere arbitrary opinions based on experience alone. But similarly, we have only to consider metaphysics, to see that, if it is to extend our knowledge at all, it can only do so by containing the same principle as its basis. For the mere analysing of conceptions already possessed can never do more than elucidate our knowledge ; if we are to extend knowledge and get beyond experience, solving such questions as whether the world has a beginning or has existed from eternity, etc., we can only do so by possessing synthetical propositions a priori ; and upon whether or not these are possible, and if so, how they are possible, depends the validity or otherwise of metaphysics. No doubt the non-progressive marches and counter-marches of philosophers prevent us from regarding metaphysics as a science, says Kant; but, there is no denying its existence as a natural disposition of the mind; and, accordingly, it is quite justifiable to ask: " How is metaphysics as a natural disposition possible? In other words, how, from the nature of universal human reason, do those questions arise which pure reason proposes to itself, and which it is impelled by its own feeling of need to answer as well as it can?" Kant contends that the only mode of solving this question, or of testing with accuracy how far the mind is capable of dealing with metaphysical problems at all, is to take those sciences where we have genuine knowledge, mathematics and physics, and ask: How are these possible? for that they are possible is clear from the fact of their existing. If we find out, then, how the mind is constituted to make mathematics and pure physics possible, we shall be able to decide how (so far as it may be found to exist) metaphysics is possible; and further, since both pure mathematics and pure physics are dependent on synthetical propositions a priori as their fundamental principles, and metaphysics is only possible on the same principle, all three enquiries really resolve themselves into one grand question: *How are synthetical propositions a priori possible?* Provided only we can answer this problem, we shall be able to decide, not only how the mind is constituted to give the knowledge it does, but also the precise limits of such knowledge, i.e., whether it is capable of transcending experience, or if not so capable, at least how it is that mind endeavours to do so.

In this way it became clear to Kant that there arose the need of a particular science, which should determine the powers of pure reason; should determine, that is to say, that part of knowledge which is purely a priori and contains no empirical element whatsoever. Such a science would be concerned with that part of knowledge which is not so much occupied with objects as with the mode of our cognition of these objects so far as this mode of cognition is possible a priori, and to this science Kant applies the term *transcendental*. By *transcendentalism* is meant, therefore, the study of the pure a priori knowledge possessed by the mind, or the "forms" of mind, as Kant sometimes calls them, or the modes of cognition which the human mind possesses independent of the matter of experience and which are necessary to make the data of sense into experience. It is really the study of these modes of knowing which, in Kant's own words, "are conditions of the possibility of experience", i.e., the modes of knowing without which experience would not be possible.

The idea of the possibility of such a science is Kant's great philosophical discovery; he is the discoverer of the transcendental or critical method, and it is because of this discovery that philosophy now mainly divides itself into Pre-Kantian and Post-Kantian. Philosophers who try to deal with the philosophical problems without subjecting knowledge to this critical process of testing just what the mind's a priori modes of cognition are, and what part they play in knowledge, Kant calls *dogmatical;* and, as previously stated, by dogmatical he does not mean a philosophy that discards the use of reason (which would clearly be no philosophy at all) ; he means dogmatical in the sense that they use reason without reasoning about reason. The dogmatic philosopher uses notions the significance of which he has never made clear to himself, and which he has not therefore proved his right to use.

Now a complete enquiry into all a priori knowledge would be called transcendental philosophy ; but this is going further than required for the present purpose ; for such an enquiry would involve not only the synthetical a priori knowledge but also the analytical, and our only object now is to understand fully the principles of synthesis a priori, with which alone the enquiry has to do. Kant, therefore, does not call his work transcendental philosophy or even a transcendental doctrine, but only a critique, since its object is not to enlarge the bounds of our knowledge a priori but only to test its worth or worthlessness, in this way purifying our reason and shielding it against error. Synthetical propositions a priori are the only concern of such an enquiry, and these must be absolutely pure, no empirical element being admitted on any account.

So much for the science with which "The Critique of Pure Reason" is concerned. It deals mainly with the two sources of our knowledge, sense and understanding; and by the first objects are given us, by the second they are thought. In so far as the faculty of sense contains a priori representations as conditions under which alone objects are to be known, it is part of transcendental philosophy, and naturally comes first in the Critique; the other part deals with the pure conditions under which objects are thought, or the a priori modes of understanding :—the two together forming what Kant calls the Transcendental Doctrine of Elements, with which the first half of the Critique is entirely concerned. This, however, will be the work of later chapters. In this chapter we have been concerned with one thing only—showing how the issue at stake, though gigantic in its scope, yet resolved itself into one all embracing question, for the answer to which Kant was led to formulate his transcendental enquiry. To some it may seem waste of space to devote such attention to introductory matter in a book like the present, but those who understand Kant's philosophy will not take this view. They will rather realise that to try and grasp the general contents of the Critique without having a clear knowledge of what the transcendental method is, and how Kant came to formulate it, is only to confuse oneself, and often, indeed, to jump to conclusions inconsistent with all the philosopher's teachings.

PART II

THE CONSTITUTIVE PRINCIPLES OF KNOWLEDGE

CHAPTER I

TRANSCENDENTAL ÆSTHETIC

IN the last chapter it was explained how Kant's problem was to answer three questions :—
(1) How is pure mathematics possible ? (2) How is pure science of nature possible ? and (3) How is metaphysics possible ? All of which, it will be remembered, resolved themselves into one grand question—How are synthetical propositions a priori possible ?

Now for the purpose of discovering the nature of consciousness there is considerable advantage gained by reducing the issue to the one central problem ; indeed, we have only to consider how synthetical judgments a priori *are* possible, and already we can anticipate broadly the whole results of the Critique. For, first, if a judgment is synthetical, it means that it connects diverse representations ; and, secondly, if it is synthetical a priori, it means that it does this, not from experience, but through pure thought. Accordingly, whatever be the *content* of our knowledge, it is clear that, if it consists of an a priori connection of diverse representations, the *form* under which the *content* falls must be the product of the mind itself. We can only have a priori synthetic judgments because we have a priori synthetic minds, in other words; and whatever sensations are given us, they can only fall under certain necessary and universal laws because the mind in the process of consciousness has necessarily to give them certain *form*, or to unite them in certain ways by reason of its a priori modes of synthesis. It thus becomes clear that, if we are to explain how knowledge such as we have is possible, our task will be to discover the mind's a priori modes of synthesis; and in this and the ensuing chapters we shall deal with Kant's theory of knowledge, showing how by his transcendental method, or theory of the principles of a priori synthesis, he answered his three questions. We shall show how he answered the first question, as to the basis of pure mathematics, in the Transcendental Æsthetic, or doctrine of the a priori forms of sensibility; how he answered the second, How is pure science of nature possible? in the Transcendental Analytic, or doctrine of the synthetical a priori forms of thought; and finally, how he answered the third question, as to how the mind is constituted to pass beyond experience and present to itself metaphysical problems, in the Transcendental Dialectic, or the doctrine of pure Ideas. These are the giant branches of Kant's tree of knowledge, and we shall deal with each in separate chapters; but it is important to notice straight away the difference between the first two and the third, i.e. sensibility and conception, on the one hand, and the Ideas of Reason, on the other; for, whereas the former are *constitutive* principles of knowledge, i.e. make the form of knowledge what it is, the Ideas are only *regulative* principles, guiding our pursuit of knowledge and unifying our experience. In other words, the process of sensibility and conception, or the operation of the categories of the understanding on the material furnished by the senses, gives us an ordered experience; but the process of bringing this experience so ordered under higher intellectual unity and of carrying on the synthetical faculty under higher and higher conditions, until finally an attempt is made to reach the unconditioned, is an additional function of reason, by which we not only unify our knowledge but pass beyond experience and present to ourselves metaphysical problems.

Of this latter process much more anon, however. Our present task is to explain Kant's theory of the *constitutive* principles of knowledge, and the first thing here is to understand roughly his conception of the relationship of sensibility and understanding, for without this there will appear to be contradiction between the Æsthetic and the Analytic. In general opinion sensibility is regarded as giving complete perception; by it objects are given us in their complete individuality and determination, and the only purpose of conception or understanding is that of abstraction and generalisation, by which single attributes and qualities are separated from the rest and made the basis of classification. But this is not Kant's view. Though in dealing with the process of sensibility in the Transcendental Æsthetic, he seems to be holding to this opinion and contending that sensibility *in itself* gives us complete perception, this is only done to simplify matters for the time being, and when we come to the Analytic we see that much more than this is required before we can have completed perception of objects. In the Analytic we see that sensibility, far from giving us objects in their fully determined form, merely gives us a manifold of sense impressions or series of isolated feelings, and that before these can lead to the perception properly so called it is essential that the understanding should bring to bear its pure conceptions and bind the manifold of sense together in accordance with its a priori laws. Considered by itself neither sensibility nor understanding can give knowledge: in Kant's words, "Concepts without percepts are empty; percepts without concepts are blind." There are, then, two indispensable factors in all knowledge—sensibility and understanding. With the a priori conditions of the first Kant deals in Transcendental Æsthetic; with those of the second in Transcendental Analytic. And though, as stated, he appears in the Æsthetic to be contending that sensibility in itself gives completed perception, when we come to the Analytic we see that in reality this is far from the case, and that perception of objects as such is only made possible by the union of the two.

With this warning to prevent confusion, we will proceed straight away with the Transcendental Æsthetic. Now in Transcendental Æsthetic Kant is dealing with sensibility, and seeking to discover its a priori conditions. The question here is: are there in perception, as distinguished from conception, any universal principles which all our perception is subject to? Can we say, prior to perceiving, that everything to be perceived will necessarily manifest certain laws? If we answer in the affirmative, then we are capable of anticipating certain elements in all our perception, and since we certainly cannot anticipate universal principles of the *sensation* given us, what we are anticipating must be based on the very nature of sensibility itself. In other words, so far as the sensation given us is concerned we are passive—we cannot tell anything about it until we receive it; consequently, if in all perception we find universal principles such that, prior to perception, we can predicate of all perception, then we must be speaking not of the sensation, the a posteriori element in perception, but of the mode of sensibility, or the a priori element under which all that is perceived must necessarily fall. Drawing a line between these two elements of perception, we may call the one the *matter* of perception, the other its *form*. And the question, therefore, is: are there, independent of all conceptions of the understanding, any *pure forms* of perception which everything perceived must fall under?

Kant answers that there are such forms of pure perception—space and time. Even when we subtract all conceptions of the understanding, such as the conceptions of cause, substance, etc., and regard objects simply as objects of perception alone, there still remain certain universal determinations in respect of them quite independent of what is given in sensation or their matter. For every object of outer-perception is *here* in a particular part of space, and *now* at a particular period of time—they are, in short, determined in space and time in reference to other objects; and likewise our states of consciousness, though not in space, can at any rate only be apprehended as determined with reference to each other in time. In perception, then, we apprehend every object, when an external object, as occupying a particular part of space; and we apprehend all objects, whether external or internal (i.e. states of consciousness), as occupying a definite point of time. Yet space and time cannot be given us in sensation, says Kant; on the contrary, they must be methods the mind has of arranging the *matter* that is given to it. On the one hand, "it is arranged in an external world, a world that is different from the mind that apprehends it." This is a world in space. On the other hand, "it is arranged as occupying a definite point of time, i.e. as occupying a certain place in the series of states constituting our inner life." This is a world in time. Space and time are therefore respectively forms of outer and inner perception. We cannot perceive anything as existing *outside* us except by putting it in certain spatial relations with other things; nor can we perceive anything *within* us, as part of our conscious states, except by placing it in certain relations of time to other states. And since all outer perceptions are states of consciousness, and therefore come under the inner sense as well as the outer sense, they are necessarily not only in space but also in time.

So much by way of introduction to Kant's theory of space and time; but, to be more accurate, what are space and time? Are they substances, actual things existing on their own account? Are they qualities or relations of things, such as would attach to them independent of our perception? Or, finally, are they conditions or forms of our perception of things, and, consequently, of the subjective conformation of our minds, without which they could not be predicated of anything? In order to satisfactorily decide this matter, and to establish them as respectively forms of the inner and outer sense, as already suggested, Kant embarks upon both a *metaphysical* and *transcendental* exposition of space and time. In the first, he seeks to show from a discussion of their nature that they are a priori representations, also what kind of a priori representations (perceptions or conceptions); and in the second, he endeavours to prove that the conclusions arrived at are the only ones that can account for the possibility of knowledge and experience such as we actually have it.

Metaphysical Exposition of Space and Time

The metaphysical exposition involves two main questions. Here Kant first considers whether space and time are a priori or a posteriori, involved in the nature of the knowing subject as indispensable conditions of consciousness or the result of impressions made on the subject from without. Then, having decided they are a priori representations, he goes on to ask, what kind of a priori representations? Are they perceptions or conceptions, products of sensibility or of understanding?

With regard to the first question, Kant's first point is that space and time cannot be derived from experience because they are logically prior to experience; indeed, all attempts to explain space and time as notions formed from experience necessarily presuppose the very thing which it is sought to explain. A consideration of the empirical view will make this clear. According to this, the ideas of space and time originate as concepts in general do. From a number of individual things sensuously perceived we abstract the attributes common to all, and thus form a concept—as, for instance, the concept redness results from perceptions of a number of red things, or the concept *man* from abstracting those attributes common to all men. In the same way, it is contended that the ideas of space and time are the result of induction from sensuous impressions themselves extended in space and time. We perceive all objects as they exist (1) out of us and beside one another, and (2) as being either simultaneous or successive; and from these perceptions we abstract what they have in common, i.e. (1) being without and beside one another, and (2) being together or after one another. From (1) we form the general concept of space, from (2) the general concept of time; and so, on this theory, space and time would be formed like all other abstract concepts. But Kant's objection to this is that the argument necessarily presupposes the very thing it would explain. We perceive things without and beside one another means nothing but that we perceive things as in space; we perceive things as simultaneous or successive means nothing but that we perceive them as in time. What we perceive, then, are things existing in space and time; and the empirical explanation really says nothing more than this: that we perceive things in space and time, and from that we abstract space and time. In other words, from space and time we abstract space and time! The argument explains the thing by itself: what is to be explained is not explained, but presupposed.

Accordingly, Kant points out that all explanations of space and time from experience are worthless, for space and time are *logically* prior to experience. When I perceive things as *out of me* (occupying a different part of space from that which my body occupies) or as out of other things (occupying a different part of space from them), I am always presupposing the space in which the localisation is made. And, likewise, when I date anything as a state of consciousness as either before or after other states of consciousness, I am presupposing the time in which the states are arranged in connection with each other. In short, the perception of objects in space and time, *as far as the logical relation of ideas goes*, implies and presupposes space and time. Hence the cognitions of space and time cannot be derived from experience, but, on the contrary, experience is only possible through the said cognitions.

The next point Kant advances in proof that space and time are a priori representations, and not derived from experience, is that they are inseparable from our intelligence. We can easily think away all objects existing in space and time, he states, but we can never think away space and time themselves. Though we can think of space without objects, we cannot conceive of the non-existence of space ; though we can conceive that nothing should occur, we cannot conceive of the non-existence of time. Space and time are therefore inseparable from our intelligence. They are a priori forms of consciousness, constituting conditions of the possibility of objects of external and internal sense, and consequently nothing can be perceived without falling within them.

From these two points—their logical priority to experience and the fact that they are inseparable from our intelligence—we see, then, that space and time are a priori representations, elements contributed by the mind itself and not notions gained from objects considered by themselves. But if they are elements contributed by the mind itself, we still have to consider what faculty of mind they are derived from, whether they are products of sense or of understanding. Now the human mind is capable of two sorts or classes of representations. On the one hand, a representation may be an individual object ; on the other, it may be a universal one. This man, this tree, this metal is an individual object ; it can only be sensuously represented or perceived. The genus man, tree, or metal is a universal object : it is abstracted from individual objects, formed from their common features ; in a word, conceived. Which of these two possible representations are space and time ? Are they percepts or are they concepts ? Now every concept, as opposed to the individual existent, consists only of the individual's essential attributes. If, for instance, we say " Shakespeare was a man ", all we mean is that Shakespeare had those attributes contained in the genus man ; but, as we know, he had many more than this. Hence it is clear that space and time could only be concepts if they were partial representations, attributes of spaces and times. But as a matter of fact just the opposite is the case : they are not partial, but the whole representation. Space contains all spaces, time all times. We do not get the ideas of space and time from making abstraction of various individual spaces and times, as, for instance, we get the conception of redness from seeing various red things; on the contrary, these particular spaces and times are only to be thought of as parts of the all embracing space and time. As Kant expresses it, "we can conceive only a single space, and when we speak of spaces, we mean only parts of one and the same sole space. These parts cannot precede the one all comprehending space as though they were the particulars from which it is generalized; but, on the contrary, they are only thought of *in* it." And the same applies to time. Consequently, space and time are not general concepts but intuitions.

Again, additional proof that space and time are intuitions and not concepts is given by their infinite magnitude. By their very nature they exceed every definite limit. No one can represent to himself a maximum of space, a space that is not contained in a greater; nor can anyone represent to himself a minimum space, a space which does not contain a lesser space. A maximum or a minimum space is an impossibility: the one always permits of being increased, the other of being diminished. And the same is true of time. Every moment follows or is followed by another. There is neither a first moment to which no other is antecedent, nor a last moment to which no other is consequent. Space and time are by their nature infinite quantities. Now " such limitlessness of progress can only be given in perception; for no mere conception of relations could carry with it such a principle of their infinity". "A conception must, indeed, be conceived as common to an infinite number of different possible individuals (it is their common type), which individuals, therefore, it holds *under* it; but no conception as such can be so thought as though it contains an infinite number of individuals *in* it"—on the contrary, in a concept the parts are definite and limited in number. But, as stated, it is thus that space is thought: all the parts of space are at one and the same time together in it ad infinitum. And the same applies to time. Consequently space and time are a priori perceptions or intuitions, and not concepts or notions.

To sum up the results of the metaphysical exposition, it has been shown that space and time, being (a) logically prior to experience and (b) inseparable from intelligence, must necessarily be a priori representations. Further, from the fact that they are (c) individual and not general and (d) concrete and not abstract, it is clear that they are not conceptions but perceptions. Briefly defined, space and time are a priori forms of the perception of objects as such. There are in perception two elements—the a posteriori element or *matter* of perception, and the a priori element or the *form* under which the matter when perceived must necessarily fall. Space and time belong to the latter; they are forms respectively of outer and inner perception, and since we cannot be conscious of anything except through these forms, our world of experience necessarily becomes spatial and temporal. Of this more anon, however, when, after completing the other sections of the Æsthetic, we come to sum up the results of our enquiry.

Transcendental Exposition of Space and Time

By a transcendental exposition is meant the demonstration that from an a priori principle of cognition a number of a priori synthetic judgments necessarily follow: in the present instance, a demonstration that from the a priori space and time perception is derived the science of mathematics. In this transcendental exposition of space and time Kant reaches the culminating point of his theory as set out in the Æsthetic. Having in the metaphysical exposition come to the conclusion that space and time are a priori forms of perception, he is now endeavouring to prove the correctness of this theory by demonstrating that it is the only one that explains the possibility of a certain branch of knowledge such as we actually have it. He seeks to prove : firstly, that all branches of the science of mathematics are based on the ideas of space and time ; and secondly, that his own theory of the nature of these ideas (as a priori forms of perception) is the only theory that can account for such a science being possible.

With regard to the first point, it is fairly clear

that the mathematical sciences are based on the ideas of space and time. In Kant's words, "Geometry has for its basis the pure perception of space ; even arithmetic produces its conceptions of number by the successive addition of units in time ; and, at any rate, no one will deny that pure mechanics would be unable to produce its conceptions of motion except by means of the idea of time." In other words, the object of geometry is figure, or magnitude of space, of which the fundamental basis is space ; the object of arithmetic is number, and numbers are formed by counting—the successive addition of unit to unit based on the fundamental condition of time ; the object of mechanics is motion or change of place, which is temporal succession in space, and therefore based on nothing but space and time together. Thus, space is the only condition of geometry, time of arithmetic, space and time together of mechanics.

Going on to the second point—that the ideas of space and time on which mathematics is based are a priori perceptions—this might already be inferred from the discussion of the nature of mathematical judgments contained in the Introduction to the Critique. It was there shown that in these three sciences we make judgments which are synthetical, intuitive, and a priori. Accordingly, if this be so, and such judgments are all based on the ideas of space and time, it is easy to see what space and time must be to give such judgments. For such judgments could not be synthetical if space

TRANSCENDENTAL ÆSTHETIC 59

and time themselves were not syntheses; they could not be intuitive in their nature if space and time were not intuitions; and they could not be a priori if space and time were not pure (and not empirical) intuitions. Thus, accepting this theory of the nature of mathematical judgments, we find ourselves driven to Kant's theory that space and time are a priori intuitions or perceptions.

But this is somewhat sweeping, as it assumes rather than proves the correctness of the statement in the introduction to the Critique, that mathematics consist of synthetical judgments a priori; so to be more accurate in proving that the mathematical sciences, admittedly based on the ideas of space and time, necessarily show these ideas to be a priori perceptions, Kant now produces two points: first, that such sciences could not be such as they are if based on conceptions and not perceptions; and secondly, that they could not carry the necessity and universality they do unless such perceptions were a priori and not empirical. As far as the first point is concerned, Kant explains that the judgments of the mathematical sciences are not developed by analysis of the ideas of space and time: on the contrary, they are products of a long process of synthesis, by which new elements are constantly being added to the ideas from which these sciences start; and only on the supposition that space and time are perceptions of sense can we explain how such synthesis is possible. For this process of synthesis by which new elements are constantly added implies that we are constantly returning to sense to add to our conceptions, much as in empirical science we constantly return to experience to add to our conceptions formed from previous experience. On these grounds, then, Kant contends that ideas of space and time from which mathematics are derived must necessarily be perceptions; but the next question is what kind of perceptions—empirical perceptions (perceptions dependent on experience alone) or a priori perceptions (perceptions involved in the nature of our perceiving faculties)? Kant answers that they must necessarily be the latter and not the former is shown by the necessity and universality mathematics carries; for how, if mathematics were not based on a priori perception, were not derived from the very nature of our perceptive faculties, could we spin out of our heads rules which all objects when perceived must necessarily fall under? If mathematical judgments were based on empirical perceptions, the most we could say about them would be: *That is what common observation tells us;* but not: *That is what, of necessity, must be*—they would not be necessary, but arbitrary, like other judgments of experience. But the mathematician, starting from pure perceptions, goes on constructing figures in space quite independent of experience, and he is sure that the figures he constructs by this purely a priori process will apply to all experience, will be universal truths. In short, in pure perception, he anticipates empirical perception with apodeictic certainty; " he perceives a priori ". How can this be? Obviously only if the space and time perceptions from which all his results are derived are pure perceptions into which all that is perceived must fall. Indeed, if this were not so, geometry, far from being an apodeictic science applying to experience, would be a mere elaborate piece of imagination having no objective validity. But on the contrary, if, as is in fact the case, all geometrical and arithmetical propositions determine the properties of space and time synthetically and with absolute necessity, so that all experience agrees with them, then it is clear that the ideas of space and time on which they are based must be a priori forms of all perception. For if space and time are the forms of outer and inner perception under which all phenomena must fall, then it is obvious that all mathematical judgments derived from such a priori forms must necessarily apply to all experience, and, as far as its form is concerned, be able to anticipate all experience with apodeictic certainty.

From the above it will be seen, then, that in this transcendental exposition of space and time Kant is further proving his conclusion arrived at in the metaphysical exposition. He is demonstrating that by accepting that conclusion, and taking space and time to be a priori forms of perception, we have a doctrine in theory of knowledge, and in fact the only doctrine, that will explain how the science of mathematics is possible. In all branches of mathematics are contained synthetical judgments a priori, judgment not derived from experience yet applying to all experience. How is this possible? Kant answers only if the ideas of space and time from which mathematical judgments are derived are pure perceptions; and that they are of this nature he seeks to prove by two points. First, by showing that mathematical judgments are synthetical and not analytical, and that only by continually resorting to sense perception can this synthesis be explained; and, secondly, by reminding us that without these perceptions were a priori perceptions and not empirical perceptions, it would be impossible to understand the necessity and universality all mathematical judgments carry. In brief, his contention is that if we recognise that space and time are pure forms of perception, then we can see that all judgments derived from these forms, though coming a priori out of the head, must necessarily apply to experience; for just as all experience is only possible under these forms, so the judgments derived from them must also be in accordance with these forms, and thus enable us to anticipate all experience, as far as its form is concerned, with apodeictic certainty.

Conclusions of the Æsthetic

Having completed both the metaphysical and transcendental exposition of space and time, we are now able to answer the question with which we started. Space and time are not real things existing on their own account, nor are they qualities or relations of real things. For if they were real things considered independent of perception, or the qualities or relations of such real things, we should only know them in actual experience, and could never anticipate them as we do in mathematics. As Kant expresses it, " neither absolute nor relative determinations of things can be perceived in anticipation of the existence of the things to which they belong." What is known in anticipation of experience must be due to the nature of the knowing subject, and can therefore only be true of phenomena, of things as they are known under the forms of consciousness, and in no sense whatever true of them as they are in themselves. Space and time, therefore, are only forms of sense perception—forms under which all phenomena must necessarily fall. Space is the form of external perception, and hence the formal condition of all external phenomena ; time is the form of internal perception, and hence the formal condition of all internal phenomena, i.e. of knowledge of our own self and our own inner states. Further, as all cognitions, whether of external or internal objects, are states of consciousness, and therefore brought under the formal condition of inner perception, it follows that time is an a priori condition of all sense-perception, immediately of internal (the soul) and mediately (i.e. through it) of external perception. Hence, just as in the external reference, I can say, *All external perceptions are in space and a priori determined according to the relations of space ;* so, in the internal reference, I can equally say, *All perceptions whatever (all objects of the senses) are in time, and fall necessarily under relations of time.* And this being so, it is easy to understand how geometry and arithmetic, being based on these forms, apply to all experience and enable us to anticipate the rules of its form with apodeictic certainty.

We now see that it is only from the standpoint of human consciousness that we can speak of space or extended substances, or of things permanent or changing in time. Directly we take away the subjective conditions under which alone perception is possible to us, the expressions space and time are meaningless. Remove the knowing subject, or even the space and time perception or intuition from the mind, and space and time relationships would vanish from the world altogether. They are only of objective validity with regard to objects of our senses, objects as known through perception; but such validity disappears directly we abstract from those modes of consciousness peculiar to us, i.e. directly we speak of things in themselves. We cannot say, therefore, " All *things* are in space and time," for such expression would apply to things as they are in themselves, apart from the mode and condition of the perception of them: all we can say is, " All *phenomena*, all *things as known in perception*, are in space and time " (meaning that *all* phenomena are in time, and *external* phenomena are also in space). Accordingly, the question of how real space and time are depends entirely on whether we are speaking of things in themselves or of phenomena, things as known in perception. If we are speaking of things in themselves, things independent of the mind, space and time are entirely ideal; they have no objective validity either as substances, or as attributes or as relations. But if we are speaking of phenomena, things as they are known in perception, space and time are real; for without them phenomena could not exist at all. As Kant expresses it, space and time are *empirically real*, but *transcendentally ideal*: meaning that, though they are real from the standpoint of ordinary consciousness, real as necessary conditions by which alone our experience becomes possible, yet if we take away the a priori conditions of perception and the part it plays in forming phenomena, we shall find that space and time are entirely ideal and have no existence independent of mind.

Finally, Kant notes that outside space and time there are no other subjective perceptions which are a priori objective, and warns us to be careful, therefore, not to seek to illustrate the ideality of space and time by the subjective character of such determinations of objects as taste, smell and colour. These latter (as such) are rightly recognised to be of subjective nature, but what a vast difference between these and space and time! For, even though agreeing with space and time in this, that they belong merely to the subjective nature of the particular form or mode of sense, it is clear that no ideality attaches to them; we cannot, as in the case of space and time, derive synthetic a priori propositions from them. In other words, the a priori space and time perception gives us universal and necessary truth; independent of the sensation given in each particular experience, it enables all minds to anticipate the form of experience in similar fashion and with apodeictic certainty. Whereas, on the contrary, such modes of sense as taste, smell and colour are always a posteriori to the sensation given, and depending, moreover, on the special character and state of the subject that perceives them, they differ with different people, and even with the same person at different times. They are thus quite incapable of anticipating experience or of giving universal and necessary truths, and if we seek to illustrate our ideality of space and time by them, we shall fall into grievous errors.

This exhausts what is significant to Kant's theory of space and time as set out in the Æsthetic. Before completing this part of the Critique it is true that he goes on to confirm his doctrine by contrasting it with the two other chief doctrines of his time—the doctrine held by Newton and generally supported by mathematical physicists of that time, that space and time are realities existing on their own account; and the doctrine of Leibniz, that they are only confused ideas of the relation of things in co-existence and succession. He illustrates the weakness of both these doctrines in very striking fashion, and also answers a number of supposed objections to his own theory. But in an exposition like the present there is nothing to be served by going into this work, which would probably tend to confuse the reader rather than elucidate the doctrine under consideration. It is, however, worth while repeating the warning given at the beginning of the chapter: that, though the Æsthetic states that " objects are given through sense ", and might easily be taken to mean that sensibility alone provides perception of objects in their complete individuality and determination, this is only done to simplify matters at a certain stage of the argument and is really far from the case. Indeed, when we come to the Analytic, we shall see that much more than this is required before we can have completed objects of perception or even (in certain senses) the space and time in which they are. In the Analytic we are shown that sensibility, far from giving us objects in their fully determined form, merely gives us a manifold of sense impressions or series of isolated feelings, and that before these can lead to perception properly so called, it is essential that there should be brought to bear the spontaneous activity of the understanding, which unconsciously synthesises or puts together the manifold of sense in accordance with its a priori laws. Indeed, Kant makes this perfectly clear when speaking of the process of uniting the manifold of sensuous impressions in the Analytic. He there says: " the combination of the many into one can never come into our minds through sense, nor can it be contained in the pure form of sensible perception and introduced along with it. It is an act of mental spontaneity ; and as we call this spontaneity understanding to distinguish it from sense, so all combination, be it conscious or unconscious, be it a combination of the manifold elements of perception or of different conceptions, and in the former case, be it a combination of pure or of sensible perception, is an act of the understanding. To this act we give the general name of synthesis in order to indicate definitely that we can represent nothing as united in the object unless we have first ourselves combined it, and that of all ideas combination is the one which cannot be given by objects but must be developed by the subject itself because it is an act of self-activity."

This is foreshadowing the Analytic, however. In the Æsthetic we are really only concerned with perception so far as its space and time element is concerned, and for the time being it is sufficient to notice that space and time are the formal characters of the process of sense perception, and as knowledge involves sense perception as an indispensable basis, all our knowledge is bound up with the conditions of space and time. The forms are all-embracing, in a word, and human experience can never get outside them.

CHAPTER II

GENERAL SURVEY OF THE ANALYTIC

THE DISCOVERY OF THE CATEGORIES

IN Transcendental Æsthetic we dealt with the a priori or transcendental conditions of sensibility, and it was shown that these were space and time, and that therefore all experience was only possible under the conditions of space and time. In like manner, in the Transcendental Analytic Kant is concerned with the a priori or transcendental conditions of understanding, and it is in this part of the Critique that he finds the answer to his second question: How is pure science of nature possible?

As explained in the second chapter, in physics or science of nature are contained propositions that carry necessity and universality, and in Kant's view such judgments could not possibly have come from experience, as no empirical judgment carries such necessity and universality. They are the a priori synthetical propositions with which we were concerned before, and in this part of the Critique Kant is applying his transcendental method to discover how many of them there are and how the mind is constituted to give them. To put the matter in other words, Kant sees that when the scientist expresses certain propositions about nature—for instance, that " every change has its cause ", " in all changes of the material world the quantity of matter remains unchanged ", and in fact, in all applications of mathematics to the concrete world—he expresses propositions that carry necessity and universality ; indeed, the scientist in going to work to solve scientific problems knows such principles beforehand and takes them with him as necessary principles for his guidance. Now, in Kant's opinion, it is impossible for such necessary principles to have come from experience ; hence he is now asking, whence do they come ? On what does their validity depend ? Obviously there is only one alternative : if the principles do not come from experience, they must come from mind. In other words, unless nature gives the principles to mind, mind must give the principles to nature ; must, that is to say, itself constitute nature in accordance with its a priori modes of judging, and nature independent of mind cannot have any existence as such.

As when dealing with space and time, Kant meets the difficulty by a further application of the distinction between *Matter* and *Form*. A priori determinations about nature will only be possible, he says, if they are concerned with the *form* of nature as opposed to the *matter*. The *matter* of experience is the variety of phenomena consisting of sensations received in space and time, and certainly this matter must have an existence independent of the understanding; but Nature is more than a variety of phenomena. To quote the late Professor Robertson, "it is a complex of objects in fixed relations with one another, of objects connected and bound together according to necessary laws. Otherwise expressed, Nature is the complex of objects of experience constituted through or according to fixed laws. Formally, it is a system of laws. These laws, in so far as necessary—which is to say, the *form* of experience—cannot be acquired as the matter of experience is. The only alternative is that the form must be innate—that the necessary laws of experience spring from the mind; and that experience, in the full and effective sense that is meant when we speak of Nature, is so constituted by the mind imposing laws upon phenomena."

The above is designed to give a rough idea of the general problem of the Analytic. Obviously Kant has here set himself an enormously difficult task. To make the transcendental discovery that the mind has certain pure concepts through which alone experience is possible, and thence to postulate that nature as regards its *form* must be constituted by mind, is one thing; to explain exactly how this comes about, how the separate faculties of sense and understanding become united, and all exists for one unchanging self-conscious self, is entirely another. We are here involved in questions of extreme complexity, and only by adhering fairly closely to the various sections of the Critique will Kant's meaning be made intelligible.

To start from the commencement, the first problem this part of the Critique is concerned with is the relation of sense and understanding. It will be remembered that a warning was given on this point in the last chapter, when we pointed out that, though the Æsthetic states that " objects are given through sense ", and might easily be taken to mean that sensibility alone provides completed perception of objects, this, in fact, is far from being Kant's ultimate contention. And now, before opening the Analytic, we find Kant stating that in this part of the Critique he has to demonstrate that knowledge, far from being given by sense alone, is the product of two factors, sense and understanding, and that neither of these by itself can possibly give us the simplest knowledge. " There are two sources in the mind from which all our knowledge is derived," he says. " The first is our capacity of having mental representations awakened in us (our passive receptivity of impressions). The second is our faculty of knowing an object by means of these impressions (our spontaneity in originating conceptions). By the former an object is presented to us, by the latter the object is thought in relation to the idea thus awakened in the mind ; or, in other words, an idea, which is in itself a mere modification of consciousness, is referred to an object. Perceptions and conceptions, therefore, contribute the elements of all our knowledge ; and neither conceptions without perceptions, nor perceptions without conceptions, can give knowledge. If the receptivity of our mind

GENERAL SURVEY OF THE ANALYTIC 73

—i.e., its capacity of having ideas awakened in it when it is in any way affected—be named *sense*, the faculty by which we ourselves produce ideas, or the spontaneity of knowledge, is what is called *understanding*. We are so constituted that perception with us can never be other than sensible; in other words, it tells us nothing except the manner in which we are affected by objects. On the other hand, the faculty of thinking the object of sensible perception is understanding. Neither of these faculties of ours has any preference over the other. Without sensibility, no object could be given to us; without understanding, no object could be thought. Thoughts without content of perceptions are empty, perceptions without conceptions are blind. Hence it is as necessary to make our conceptions sensible —i.e. to find an object for them in perception, as it is to make our perceptions intelligible—i.e., to bring them under conceptions. Nor is it possible for these two faculties to exchange their functions. Understanding can no more perceive anything than the senses can think anything. Knowledge can only come of the union of the two; yet we must not on that account confuse the two distinct elements; nay, we have every reason carefully to separate and distinguish them."

Kant's meaning here has been somewhat misinterpreted by reason of different interpretations of the word " object " in such sentences as " without sensibility no object could be given us ". Sometimes the term " object " has been taken to stand for the bare manifold of sense, at other times to stand for the phenomenal object given in completed perception; but only in the former sense is the term " object " here used, and if we realise this, and remember that when Kant says " through sensibility objects are given us ", he only means a sensuous manifold is given us and not that objects are given us, his meaning becomes clear enough. We then see that through sensibility we are given nothing more than sensuous manifolds, or mental modifications, and that before these can be rendered objective and become known, it is necessary that they should be thought or synthesised by the understanding. True, bare sensations such as smell, colour, sound, etc. could be given by sensibility independent of thought; but so given they could not be perceived as they are in experience, for when perceived in experience they are referred to objects, which implies judgment, and all judging is only made possible by the understanding. Thus, sense by itself and considered as severed from the understanding, would not yield perception of objects; it would merely be a chaotic assembly of sensuary elements, and only when the understanding brings to bear certain of its pure notions or forms of synthesis on this unconnected manifold of sense is knowledge or finished perception produced.* There

* The reader might ask : Why cannot knowledge of perceived objects be accounted for solely by sensibility ? The answer may be expressed thus : Knowledge of objects manifests two distinct characters, an empirical factor and an a priori factor. So the question becomes : Why cannot Kant derive a priori factors from empirical factors and thus retain sensibility alone, or vice versa ?

are, then, two separate faculties involved in knowledge : *sensibility*, the mind's capacity of receptivity, which may be regarded as the intuitive element ; and *understanding* or thought, which may be regarded as the discursive element. Distinguishing these two factors, the theory of the rules of Sensibility is *Æsthetic*, which we have already dealt with ; the theory of the rules of the Understanding is *Logic*, to which we now turn.

THE TWO LOGICS. INTRODUCTION TO THE ANALYTIC

Dealing with logic, Kant first draws a parallel between general Logic and the new Transcendental logic he is about to explain. Pure general Logic, he tells us, is a science that deals with the form of thought. By analysing concepts it determines the process of thought so far as it is the same for all ideas and concepts, and thus reveals the absolutely necessary rules of thought without which there can be no proper employment of the understanding at

The answer is : (1) A priori (i.e. universal and necessary predicates), cannot be derived from sense manifolds by induction (cf. Part II, Chap. I, p. 51 ff. in the case of spatial and temporal predicates) ; but it is undeniable that our experience *does* contain these universal factors ; therefore Kant thinks they must derive from a cognitative faculty which is qualitatively different from sensibility. Further (2), as Berkeley had pointed out, the sensuary manifold comes to us " willy nilly " ; the mind is entirely receptive in regard to it, and this receptivity is an essential characteristic of sensibility as defined by Kant. Now, as we have seen, the central contention of the whole Critique is that knowledge is fundamentally synthetic. But synthesis is a combining, and therefore an *active* mode of cognition ; thence it follows, since one and the same faculty cannot be both active and passive, that there is a faculty additional to sensibility, and this is understanding or thought.

all. Here the only problem is how the mind relates its ideas to each other; the process is analytic, proceeding according to the principles of identity and contradiction, and the question of the origin of what is analysed is not gone into. But it is possible, says Kant, to imagine another kind of logic, a logic not merely analytic but synthetic, which would reveal the mind's conditions of forming cognitive judgments, or the origin of knowledge so far as it is due to the mind itself. Indeed, just as we found in Transcendental Æsthetic that there is pure as well as empirical perceptions, so we may find that there is pure as well as empirical thought of objects; and if this be so, we should have a " logic which would relate to the origin of our actual perceptions and other cognitions of objects of experience so far as that origin did not lie in the objects themselves." In other words, Kant's meaning is that, independent of the *matter* for consciousness and the a priori conditions of sensibility, there may be a priori thought-functions, forms of pure synthesis essential to the consciousness of anything. If so, a science of these forms would enable us, up to a certain point, to determine objects a priori, for it would lay down the universal and necessary rules of the understanding without which nothing could be known. Further, such a logic would supply the long sought after criterion of truth. Not a criterion of all truth, it is true: this is impossible, for the *matter* of consciousness cannot be but empirically got. But if there be universal and necessary rules of the understanding without which no object can be known, it is clear that whatever contradicts these is false, inasmuch as the understanding would then contradict its own universal rules of thought and consequently its own self. In contradistinction to general logic, such a logic might be called Transcendental Logic, for transcendental is the word we use to denote a priori ideas having objective meaning or enabling us to know objects.

Now just as pure general logic contains three divisions, dealing respectively with apprehension, judgment, and reasoning, so Kant holds that transcendental logic has a parallel for each of these. First, corresponding to the part of general logic dealing with apprehension, we have the a priori thought functions, or the conceptions of objects in general derived from the understanding; secondly, corresponding to the part dealing with judgment, we have the principles of judgment which come about when the pure conceptions of the understanding are applied to the pure and empirical factors given in sensibility; and thirdly, corresponding to reasoning in general logic, we have certain supreme principles of connection amongst judgments, giving systematic union to all our knowledge and experience. There are thus three branches of Transcendental Logic. The first two of these branches constitute the *Transcendental Analytic*, which divides itself into two parts. The first part (corresponding to the part of pure general logic dealing with apprehension) is the *Analytic of Con-*

ceptions, which analyses the understanding to discover the pure conceptions or forms of synthesis it contains, and then proceeds to justify these by showing that they are the identical conceptions required for or presupposed in our actual knowledge or experience. The second part (corresponding to the part of pure general logic dealing with judgment) is the *Analytic of Principles*, and this analyses the principles all experience falls under, or demonstrates the principles of judgment the mind gives rise to when the pure conceptions of the understanding are applied to the pure and empirical factors given in sensibility. This constitutes one main division of the Critique, and it covers all the constitutive principles of knowledge. But going on to reasoning, just as in general logic we pass from the immediate connection of perceptions in judgment to their mediate connection in syllogism, so Kant seeks to show that in Transcendental Logic we find certain supreme principles of connection amongst judgments, giving systematic unity to all our knowledge and experience, and these give rise to the Transcendental Dialectic. This latter division of the Critique is scarcely theory of knowledge, however; on the contrary, it deals with the limits of knowledge, exposing the illusions by which we fancy we can pass beyond those limits. Kant uses the word dialectic in the sense in which the ancients used it, as meaning a logic of false show, and is concerned with the outcome of using the pure conceptions of the understanding beyond experience. Applied to what is given in sense, such conceptions of the understanding certainly have objective validity, for it is impossible for us to have any experience without their use : they are the conditions by which alone objects as such can be thought, and therefore constitute a logic of truth for all experience. But it is very tempting to use these pure principles by themselves, beyond experience, i.e., independent of the *matter* for consciousness ; and in this way, out of its own formal principles, the understanding makes mere cobwebs of reason, ideas in relation to which there cannot be any objective reality, because a sensuary manifold is not a constituent of such ideas. Kant calls such use of reason dialectic, and the Transcendental Dialectic consists of a demonstration of this transcendent use of the understanding and reason, in order to detect its groundless pretensions and keep it within its correct bounds. Transcendental Dialectic, however, will constitute a separate part of this book ; at present, in sketching an outline of the Critique, we need only note that it is one of the branches of Transcendental Logic corresponding to the three divisions of general Logic.

This general survey of the Transcendental Logic will be sufficient to convey the general scheme of the Critique. It will be seen that in effect Kant is saying : through sensibility alone we can only receive sensuous manifolds, mere modifications of consciousness, and before there can be knowledge it is necessary that these should be thought or conceived, the conditions of this type of knowledge being called Transcendental Logic, which divides itself into three branches. But before we proceed to Kant's exposition of the first of these branches, it will perhaps make matters clearer to consider the part thought plays in perception generally, also to foreshadow what Kant is about to prove. As to the first, we have only to consider the simplest act of perception to see that passive perception does not exist, but that activity of thought or conception is present in all our perception. For instance, if I open my eyes at any moment, what I am actually given in sense are so many sensations, but what I *perceive* is something more than bare sensuary elements. I do not merely perceive qualities of objects; I perceive chairs, tables, books, etc., each of which represents a number of different qualities combined in a determinate manner. In other words, I am capable of describing or classifying the content of my perception; the separate qualities of the continuous whole given to me, are grouped together or synthetically united. This, in fact, is what is involved when I say, for example, " That is a horse "; I have taken all the perceived qualities and formed a concept, and the thought " that is a horse " involves that various qualities perceived at different times—having four legs, running, eating grass, etc.—have been united under one concept. Hence, in Kant's words, " Concepts depend on functions. By function I mean the unity of the act of arranging different representations under one common representation." And, in Kant's opinion, the reason the objects perceived are at once understood by us is because it is only by certain pure conceptions of the understanding that we are able to perceive at all. From his standpoint, concepts are modes of arranging the sensuous manifold as brought under the forms of intuition; and we now understand what he means when he says: "Perceptions without conceptions are blind—Thoughts without content are empty." In other words, without the faculty of understanding, sensibility alone would not constitute knowledge; but, on the other hand, without sensibility thought would have no material to arrange.

Now many of our concepts are empirical. We get them from observing likenesses and differences in what we perceive, and observing what is essential and what is accidental. With these empirical concepts Kant is not specially concerned. But there are certain concepts—categories, as Kant calls them—which stand as indispensable and ultimate factors in the ordering and arranging of experience and of the concepts of experience—concepts which science, though never proving their validity, always presupposes as principles in going to work. These are the grounds of all the synthetic judgments with which we were concerned before, and Kant holds that it is because of such categories that our experience is an ordered one, phenomena always connected and related in certain ways, and not merely arbitrary, differing among individuals.

When, for example, I perceive a stone as hot and correctly infer that the sun is the cause of the heat in the stone, I am expressing a judgment that is objective, necessary and universal: it is a scientific judgment; all stones similarly related to the sun will also be hot. Such judgments as these are not merely empirical, Kant contends; they are due to certain thought-functions lying a priori in the seat of the understanding, and in the Analytic he is concerned with discovering what are these functions of unity or pure forms of synthesis constituting the understanding, and how they serve to constitute experience. To understand, he states, is to unite in consciousness, and these forms of unity are the categories, whose function is to unite sense presentations in certain necessary ways, thereby referring them to one unchanging self-conscious self. By these categories or unifying factors the various sensations or unconditioned modifications of consciousness become formed into unities, orders, sequences, identities; and thus, out of what is given in sense, we represent to ourselves objects and the ordered experience called nature. It is with constituting the mere manifold of sense into a systematic unity of experience existing for a self-conscious self that Transcendental Analytic is concerned with. Taking the Analytic as a whole, the problem is: How can pure concepts become fundamental principles of experience? And the starting point is the discovery of the categories, the conclusion the fundamental principles they give rise to when applied to the sensuary manifold in space and time.

So much for the general field Kant is about to cover in the Analytic. As stated before, it divides itself into two main divisions—*Analytic of Conceptions* and *Analytic of Principles*, which in Transcendental Logic Kant contends respectively correspond to the parts of general logic dealing with apprehension and with judgment. The first is a statement of the ultimate forms to which the unifying process of intelligence may be reduced; the second exhibits these elements of unification as syntheses in the concrete world itself. *Analytic of Conceptions* is subdivided into :—(1) *The Metaphysical Deduction of the Categories*, an analysis of the understanding to discover how many categories or pure forms of synthesis it contains and uses to determine the objects of experience; (2) *The Transcendental Deduction of the Categories*, in which it is sought to show that the pure conceptions discovered in the above are the identical categories which are needed for, and presupposed in, our actual knowledge or experience. In like fashion, *Analytic of Principles* is subdivided into :—(1) *The Schematism of the Categories*, showing how the purely intellectual categories become so expressed as to enable the sensuous manifold to become subsumed under them; and (2) *The Principles of the Understanding*, which is a statement of the universal judgments in relation to objects of experience which it is possible to make when we apply the schematised categories to what is given in perception. To the first of these branches, the *Metaphysical Deduction of the Categories*, we proceed straightaway; the *Transcendental Deduction* and the *Analytic of Principles* will be dealt with in separate chapters.

THE METAPHYSICAL DEDUCTION OF THE CATEGORIES

As previously stated, this part of the Critique is an analysis of the understanding to discover how many pure conceptions or forms of syntheses it contains and uses to determine the objects of experience. Before making such analysis Kant points out that there are three main requirements to be borne in mind: first, that the conceptions be pure and not empirical; second, that they belong to thought or understanding, and not to intuition or sensibility; and third, that they are primitive conceptions, and not deduced or compound conceptions.

Now in the comparison of general logic and Transcendental Logic set out above we saw that the former revealed to us the characteristic of the understanding so far as it deals with the objects given to it. We saw that its work consists in reducing varity to unity or in comprehending individuals under classes, in this way connecting them together. How the objects it deals with originate it does not concern itself with; it simply takes ideas of objects in their concrete individuality and connects them together by abstraction and generalization. In fact, in the eyes of general logic the work of the

GENERAL SURVEY OF THE ANALYTIC

understanding simply lies in comparing the individuals, observing their common elements, abstracting from their differences, and so subsuming them under generic concepts; and this process of analytical unity can be continued until at last we reach the unity of all things in the abstract conception of an object in general. Now if objects were given us in their concrete individuality by sense alone, this process would certainly be sufficient to exhaust the complete function of the understanding; but, as we have seen, in Kant's view sensibility does not give us objects in their concrete individuality, which is the stage from which general logic starts : all it gives us is an unconnected manifold; and before we can attain to the objects of completed perception, the isolated data of sense must be synthesised or united into a concrete whole. Hence, before the analysis with which ordinary logic is concerned, and the secondary synthesis to which that analysis leads, there must be a primary synthesis; and since, as we have seen, of the two faculties of knowledge, sense and understanding, only the activity of the latter can give unity, it follows that the principles of this synthesis must lie in the understanding itself. In fact, Kant is now about to show us that the same function which is exercised by the understanding in forming the concepts of conscious judgment is also (unconsciously) exercised by it in uniting the manifold given in sense; the same faculty that ties up a number of objects, or unites lower concepts under higher ones, also ties up the manifold given in sense to form an object. Kant's theory, in short, is that in all our perception there are certain a priori conceptions of the understanding constituting the rules which it follows in putting together the manifold given in sense, and until the data of sense are arranged according to these rules they are " blind "—to beings who can only cognise through pure concepts they are absolutely nothing. The whole process of conceiving objects lies in subsuming what is given in sense under more and more general conceptions, all ultimately derived from certain pure conceptions of the understanding. It is nothing but a mode of classing lower concepts and intuitions under higher ones, which are not only capable of containing those actually subsumed under them in any particular instance, but many others; and so on all the way up the scale, until finally we reach the fundamental conceptions constituting the necessary conditions of all understanding. Thus, to take instances, our conception of a triangle serves for a rule or limiting condition under which the sensuary manifold is combined to represent a drawn triangle, and our conception of matter as extended and impenetrable serves as a rule subject to which we put together the elements in our idea of any particular body. But, if we pass higher, we find that all these relatively general conceptions as rules of syntheses are ultimately subject to the pure conceptions of the understanding, which constitute the conditions of the possibility of all conception. Ultimately, in fact, all combination

GENERAL SURVEY OF THE ANALYTIC

of different elements must rest on the conceptions of objects in general, or the fundamental modes of syntheses contained a priori in the seat of the understanding; and just as these supply the rules of synthesis for the lower conceptions, so, through these lower conceptions, they also supply the rules of synthesis by which we put together the unconnected manifold of sense.

It is this primary synthesis, uniting the manifold of sense into objects, that Transcendental Analytic is concerned with, and Kant is now seeking to discover the various forms of synthesis or functions of unity which the understanding here employs. Now, as we have seen, Kant's contention is that there are two separate faculties in our knowledge: *sensibility*, our capacity of receptivity, and *understanding*, our capacity for spontaneity of thought. Sensibility can only give us intuitions or an unconnected manifold; hence the unities which objects imply must depend on the active forms of the understanding, or on notions, as Kant calls them. Now notions, he states, can only be used by the understanding so far as it judges by them: to understand is to judge; there is no act of the understanding that cannot be reduced to a judgment. Hence, if we are to find all the forms of the understanding, we have only to gain a thorough knowledge of the nature of our judgments.

We accordingly examine the nature of our judgments, and what do we find? We find they all depend on a number of notions or pure forms of subsumption, which are the same for all judgments, no matter what the nature of the subject matter judged ; hence, if the only use that can be made of the understanding is to judge by it, it follows that the notions or pure forms of subsumption on which judgments depend must also be the forms of synthesis by which the understanding unites the unconnected manifold of sense to form the objects of experience. As Kant expresses it, "in every judgment there is a notion which comprehending several, is applied to a given one ; and this latter is directly referred then to the object. Thus, in the judgment *All bodies are divisible*, the notion of divisibility, as referable to several, is specially applied to one among these, body ; and that, again, to certain actual objects of sense. These objects, therefore, are only mediately cognised through the notion of divisibility. All judgments are, accordingly, functions of unity to the variety in a cognition: in the cognition of an object, namely, there is employed in judgment, not an immediate element (of consciousness) but a higher one comprehending immediate elements under it ; and in this manner several possible units of cognition are combined into a single one."

Kant's contention, then, comes back to this : that, since understanding is the same as judging (and, in fact, no use can be made of the understanding except so far as it judges by it), and since, further, all judgments depend on notions, if we find these notions or functions of unity in judgments, we shall have the categories of the understanding. In other words, if we want to find the different forms of syntheses which the understanding contains and uses to determine objects, we have only to analyse all our judgments, finding the ultimate notions on which they depend; and since general logic has already done this for us, we can go to it for help. There will be as many categories, or concepts of the pure understanding, as there are types of judgments in the logical table of judgments. Or, in other words, precisely in the same forms as each type of logical judgment combines its terms, so will thought combine the elements of sense in the understanding of an object. All required is to abstract the matter from any particular judgment, leaving its pure form revealed, and the logical type under which such judgment falls will be one or other of the categories.

Now if we take the complete list of logical judgments, we find that every judgment, as such, has a certain quantity, quality, relation, and modality; that is to say, subject matter apart, every judgment consists in nothing but the relation or connection of two representations in accordance with these four headings. Thus, as Kuno Fischer expresses it: " of the two representations, one (the subject) must always be contained *under* the other; every judgment represents by its predicate the circumference or magnitude of the subject: this is the *quantity* of the judgment. Of the two representations, one (the predicate) must be always contained *in* the other; every judgment represents by its predicate an attribute of the subject: this is the *quality* of the judgment. Of the two representations, one is necessarily subject, and the other predicate; it is not a matter of indifference which place either takes; there is a necessary reference of subject and predicate, which is represented in every judgment: this is its *relation*. Finally, the connexion or copula of the two representations must be cognised by us in a definite manner, and every judgment must represent this manner: this is its *modality*. The reference of the two representations to one another is determined by *quantity* (on the side of the subject); *quality* (on the side of the predicate); *relation* (reciprocally); the connexion of the two representations is determined by *modality*. These four are the recognised attributes of pure judgment."

Again, under each of these four classes there are contained three species; so that setting out the complete list, we have the following table:—

Logical Table of Judgments

1	2
According to Quantity	*According to Quality*
Singular (Napoleon was Emperor of France)	Affirmative (Heat is a form of motion)
Particular (Some plants are cryptogams)	Negative (Mind is not extended)
Universal (All metals are elements)	Infinitive (Mind is unextended)

3	4
According to Relation	*According to Modality*
Categorical (The body is heavy)	Problematical (This may be poison)
Hypothetical (If the air is warm, the thermometer rises)	Assertorial (This is poison)
Disjunctive (The substance is either fluid or solid)	Apodeictic (Every effect must have its cause)

According to Kant, these are all the forms of logical judgments, and, in accordance with all said above, it is easy to arrive at the categories or the pure forms of synthesis on which each of them depends. Thus, the forms of the singular, particular, and universal judgments gives us the Categories of quantity : Unity, Plurality, Totality. The forms of affirmation, negation, and limitation judgments gives the Categories of quality : Reality, Negation, Limitation. The forms of the categorical, hypothetical and disjunctive judgments gives us the Categories of relation : Substance and Accidents, Cause and Effect, Reciprocal Action or Reciprocity. And lastly, the forms of the problematical, assertorial, and apodeictal judgments give us the Categories of modality : Possibility and Impossibility, Existence and Non-Existence, Necessity and Contingence.

This, then, is the catalogue of all the pure forms of synthesis or thought-functions which the understanding contains a priori. If we like, we may call them conceptions of objects in general, for it is by these that the unconnected manifold of sense become united into objects, and arranged as unities, orders, sequences, identities. Aristotle, Kant points out, had searched for such a list of fundamental conceptions over 2,000 years ago, when at one stroke he came very near founding the whole science of Logic ; but the fifteen he eventually named were defective in that some of them were modes of pure sensibility, one empirical, others deduced concepts, whilst some, again, were wanting altogether. The understanding, it is true, is capable of certain pure concepts other than those set out, but these are only deduced concepts, derived from those already mentioned.

Dealing with the table set out, Kant explains that the four classes can be divided into two sides ; those that relate to the nature of objects, on the one hand, and those that relate to the existence of these objects in relation to one another, or to the understanding, on the other. The former class he calls the *mathematical*, the latter the *dynamical* categories. Again, it is interesting to note that the number of the categories in each class is three, whereas generally all a priori division with conceptions must be dichotomous (e.g., A or non-A), and that the third category of each three is always the result of the combination of the second with the first. Thus, " Totality is nothing else but Plurality contemplated as Unity ; Limitation is merely Reality conjoined with Negation ; Reciprocity is the Causality of a Substance, reciprocally determining and determined by other Substances ;

and finally Necessity is nothing but Existence, which is given through the Possibility itself." It must not be supposed on this account, however, that the third category is merely a deduced one, like some of Aristotle's; for the production of the third category from the first two in all cases requires a particular function of the understanding quite additional to those exercised in the first and second categories, and is therefore to be regarded as an independent conception.

This completes the discovery of the categories, and gives sufficient explanation of their nature for the time being. Were we engaged upon anything approaching a critical exposition of the philosophy, it would be necessary to show that Kant's derivation of the categories has been shown by philosophers to be open to much criticism, some of the judgments in the table of logical judgments from which he took them being very dubious, sometimes untenable, indeed. But a simple exposition is all we are now aiming at, and whatever errors the Kantian list of categories may contain, this does not necessarily diminish the philosophical importance of Kant's work, for it does not in the least show that experience may not be constituted in the fashion he has laid down, by categories of thought very similar to the Kantian. It is sufficient here to simply set out the categories as presented by Kant, and show his method of discovering them; their nature and how they constitute experience will be made clearer in later chapters.

CHAPTER III

THE TRANSCENDENTAL DEDUCTION OF
THE CATEGORIES

THIS is one of the most important parts of the Critique, for it contains what is undoubtedly the central thought in Kant's theory of knowledge, and the different forms of presentation in the first and second editions of the great work show it to be the part with which Kant found it most difficult to satisfy himself. We saw in the last section how Kant analysed the pure understanding and found it contained twelve pure conceptions or categories, which he stated served to make experience possible; he is now concerned with justifying these categories, i.e., demonstrating that they are just those categories that are required for, and presupposed in, our actual knowledge and experience; that the knowledge we have would not be possible without them.

Now jurists, he opens by remarking, distinguish in a cause the question of right from the question of fact, and give to the proof of the former the name of Deduction. Likewise, if we take the various conceptions comprising the web of human cognition and ask by what right we use them, the process of

DEDUCTION OF THE CATEGORIES

establishing such a right might be given a similar title—a deduction (or justification) of conceptions. In the case of conceptions derived from experience such a deduction would be easy enough, for in this case we could simply go to experience and point out that our right to use them was undoubted, as they had been taken from experience, and this, an empirical deduction, would be quite sufficient for our purpose. But in the case of the categories matters are very different; these are not derived from experience but are a priori, and if, therefore, we try to show how and why we can apply them to experience, we require not an empirical deduction, which can only show how conceptions are derived from experience, but a transcendental deduction, giving an explanation of why they must necessarily be in experience. In other words, to establish the objective validity of the categories we need to show that the nature of knowledge is such that, transcendentally considered, it necessarily presupposes them; that, in fact, our experience could not be such as it is without such a priori categories were used to make it such. And in the case of the categories this deduction becomes doubly necessary to philosophy because, not only do we want to show how they make experience possible, but because on the answer to this question will depend, besides their objective validity, the further question of whether they can be used beyond experience in the sense of giving us knowledge of God or immortality, for instance.

Before commencing such a deduction Kant prepares the way for it by a general survey of the question under consideration and what he is about to prove. There are, he says, only two possible ways in which perceptual objects can be accounted for: when either such completed objects are entirely derivable from the data of sense, or from the a priori conceptions. The first alternative can be dismissed, since in that case we could not possibly account for necessity in knowledge, nor would any a priori conceptions be possible. It is clear that certain conceptions are most certainly a priori, since they carry necessity and universality, and therefore, though they agree with objects, they most certainly cannot be derived from objects as such. The matter of sensible cognition is no doubt given in experience (though our knowledge of such, for instance, the sensation of colour, smell, etc., is quite different from the element in the unknown things in themselves that excites such sensations in us). But space, time, substantiality, causality, etc., do not depend on the affections that come to us. Such notions by reason of the necessity they carry are a priori forms pertaining exclusively to the subject, and are not dependent on the things in themselves, whose relations, if such there be, are necessarily quite unknown to us.

Very well, then; since the sense data alone do not make perceptual objects possible, we are driven to the second alternative, namely, that the categories make them possible; and Kant proceeds

DEDUCTION OF THE CATEGORIES

to point out that, though in this case the categories alone cannot produce the object as to its existence (i.e. the matter for consciousness cannot but be empirically got), it is quite possible that it may be a priori determinative of the ultimate object as regards its form, since it may well be that only by means of the categories is it possible for us to cognise anything as an object. In other words, it may well be that the completed phenomenon takes its laws from our a priori conceptions, and that the manifold given in sensibility cannot be constituted into an object except by being subjected to necessary principles of the understanding.

There are two conditions essential to the cognition of objects, Kant contends : first, *Intuition*, by means of which the object (though only as an inconceived manifold in space and time) is given us ; and secondly, *Conception*, by means of which what is given in intuition is thought as an object. From what was said in Transcendental Æsthetic it is clear that the first condition, the arrangement in space and time under which alone the barest perception is possible, must in fact exist, as a formal basis for it, a priori in the mind; and this formal condition of sensibility, therefore, all phenomena necessarily exemplify, because it is only in accordance with it that they can be empirically intuited. But the question now is, whether there do not also exist a priori in the mind conceptions of understanding as conditions under which that which is already intuited, is yet thought as an object. If we answer this in the affirmative, it follows that all empirical cognition of objects is necessarily conformable to such conceptions, since, if they are not presupposed, it is impossible that anything can be an object of experience. "Now all experience," Kant states, "contains besides the intuition of the senses through which an object is given, a *conception* also of an object that is given in intuition. Accordingly, conceptions of objects in general must lie as a priori conditions at the foundation of all empirical cognition; and consequently, the objective validity of the categories, as a priori conceptions, will rest upon this, that experience (as far as regards the form of thought) is possible only by their means. For in that case they apply necessarily and a priori to objects of experience, because only through them can an object of experience be thought. The whole aim of the transcendental deduction of all a priori conceptions is to show that these conceptions are a priori conditions of the possibility of all experience. Conceptions which afford us the objective foundation of the possibility of experience are for that very reason necessary." The categories, Kant contends, are these identical modes of conception. " They are conceptions of an object in general, by means of which its intuition is contemplated as determined in relation to one of the logical functions of judgment." Thus, " the function of the categorical judgment is that of the relation of subject to predicate; for example, in the proposition, ' All bodies are divisible'. But in regard to the merely logical use of the understanding, it still remains undetermined to which of these two conceptions belongs the function of subject, and to which that of predicate. For we could also say, ' Some divisible is a body'. But the category of substance, when the conception of a body is brought under it, determines that; and its empirical intuition in experience must be contemplated always as subject and never as mere predicate. And so with all the other categories."

So much by way of introduction to Kant's Deduction of the Categories; but, in addition, it is perhaps as well to remind the reader straightaway that the Critique is only concerned with necessary knowledge or unities actually found in the objective world itself, not with contingent knowledge, where phenomenal representations are merely associated by the subject and are valid only for an individual consciousness. The two processes must be kept quite distinct. On the one hand, we have the combination of two presentations in a manner valid not merely for an individual consciousness, but for every conscious subject or consciousness in general, as Kant calls it; on the other, we have merely the combination of presentations in a certain time order, the empirical ego, which itself consists simply of a sensuary manifold given to internal sense and determined in time. The former accounts for the manifold of intuition as united into an object and holds good for all consciousness, as in the perception of freezing water or the judgment "this body is heavy"; the latter is only a unity by means of association relating to a phenomenal world, and therefore only good for an individual consciousness. It is with the former alone that the following deduction is concerned; the contingent and subjective judgments in relation to the Empirical Ego are the subject matter of psychology, and the Critique, restricted as it is to universal and necessary knowledge, does not deal with them beyond making clear the distinction.

THE TRANSCENDENTAL UNITY OF APPERCEPTION

Now, expressed in rough, Kant's deduction of the categories, his proof that they must have objective validity, lies in this: he first of all shows that for consciousness of "Nature" or a world of objects all existing in necessary relationship to each other, such as we have in experience, one supreme principle of synthesis or unity of thought is required, and he then goes on to show that the manifold of sense could not possibly comply with this supreme principle except in so far as they are combined in accordance with the categories. Experience in its general outlines is always a system, it must be remembered; no matter how confused a mind a person may have, his experience is always organised in this respect at least: that all objects are represented as existing in one space (are arranged, that is to say, in definite relations of different parts of space), and all events are represented as taking place in one time (are arranged in definite relations of different parts of time). The unity of space and time is thus presupposed as conditioning all objects of experience; and the problem is, How can this world of objects, all related to each other through the one space and time in which they are included, be evolved out of the fleeting manifold of sense? how can the mere flux of sensations become transmuted into a system of permanent objects acting in definite ways on each other? The mere manifold of sense in itself would only give rise to a scattered consciousness, Kant contends, if to any consciousness at all, and the consciousness of "Nature" or the systematic unity of experience would be inexplicable. But, on the other hand, he maintains that such a consciousness can be explained by the theory he propounds, namely, a supreme principle of intelligence bringing all the manifold to a unity and using the categories as a means of doing so. The essence of our consciousness is conjunction, he holds, and all conjunction is solely due to the activity or synthesising power of the understanding. The constitution of our experience consists of a conjunction of presentations in relation to one unchanging self, or in bringing all presentations under the transcendental unity of apperception, and the only way the manifold of sense can comply with this necessity is by the operation of the categories, whose function is to bring cognitions under the unity of apperception by uniting them into judgments.

This, in rough, is Kant's proof that the categories must have objective validity, and from this it will be seen that the central thought of the deduction is the Unity of Apperception. What does Kant mean by this exactly ? Apperception, in the meaning previously used by Leibniz, is a word taken to imply self-consciousness, or rather that consciousness of self associated with all perception that seems, as it were, to stand in opposition to the objects perceived ; so that, whenever I perceive I am not only aware of the objects I perceive, but also of the self or the " I " for which such objects are. In other words, it is a consciousness that returns upon the self ; it enables me not only to be conscious of the objects but of myself in perceiving them, so that in every act of perception I am able to say : " these objects are mine ", " everything given in this perception belongs to me " ; " I am the unity to which it is all referred ".

Now Kant makes an analysis of this return upon the self, and what he maintains is that it is an outcome of the particular nature of our consciousness, by which all the manifold given in perception becomes united into a system of objects by complying with a supreme principle of thought working according to its necessary laws or categories. In other words, only because the intellect is capable of forming all my ideas into a unity, is capable of binding every element given in perception into one system of objects, can I become conscious of the one identical self throughout all changes of experience. Accordingly, whatever sense manifold is given in consciousness, it can only exist for *me*, or be known by the one self, by being determined in accordance with the categories, which involves its being united with the other parts of my consciousness and becoming a part of the whole which I call *mine*. Indeed, if any matter of consciousness did not fall under this unity and become an element in the consciousness of the one system of objects, it would either destroy the unity of self (which would mean chaos), or it would be *for me* " as good as nothing ". In other words, any failure on the part of what entered the mind to become united with other parts, and so form a whole in which all elements found their places, could only lead to two alternatives equally fatal to knowledge : in the first case, the splitting of the self would mean a complete break of connection between the two successive experiences referred to the two different selves, and experience before and after the division of the self, instead of forming parts of one experience, would refer to different worlds ; and in the second, that which did not so become weaved into the whole would lead to no consciousness at all, since it would never become part of the self's experience. In this way, Kant argues that the identity of the self necessarily demands the unity of our experience as a whole, all existing as parts of one space and one time ; or otherwise expressed, the consciousness of one unchanging self throughout all experience implies that every element in consciousness must be related to the other elements, and thus form one systematic unity of experience.

This is one end of the pole; starting with the identical self, we can lay it down that everything down to the manifold of sense must take its place as an element in the whole in order for this identical self to be possible. But even if we start at the other end, and, taking the mere manifold of sense, ask, How can this by itself lead to knowledge? we shall find ourselves forced to add various qualifications or further conditions (each necessarily presupposing the other), until finally we are again driven to the identical self. Thus, by merely receiving sense impressions, even admitting they are modified by this process, we should never get knowledge; for as merely receptive sense cannot bind the manifold together. For this something more than receptivity is required; it is essential that the manifold should be synthesised, and this process can only be attributed to the spontaneity of the understanding. Wherever, therefore, as in all our ideas of objects, there is a combination of the manifold elements given in sense, there must be an act of synthesis by the understanding to bring about the various unities; and if there are different forms of unities, there must be different forms of a priori synthesis. This is our first point, that all combination objects imply must be due to the activity of the understanding expressing itself in various forms. But next we have to recognise that the very idea of synthesis presupposes an absolute unity in relation to which it is made; that is to say, the bringing of sense impressions into unity and combination implies the putting of them into relation with a unity in consciousness that remains the same through all changes. This unity cannot be the category of unity, for that itself presupposes it, and, like the other categories or forms of synthesis, is epistemologically dependent on it. It is clearly not a conception at all, but a supreme principle of synthesis that all conceptions logically presuppose; and it is this that constitutes the unity of apperception, or the identical self conscious self with which we were concerned before. Kant often calls this pure self, the " I " that thinks, the Transcendental Ego to distinguish it from the Empirical (or object) Ego known by introspection, and, as will be made clearer later, it makes the latter possible, as it does the whole world of experience. The following passages will make Kant's meaning clearer :—" The ' *I think* ' must accompany all my representations, for otherwise something would be represented in me which could not be thought; in other words, the representation would either be impossible, or at least be, in relation to me, nothing."—" This representation, ' I think ', is an act of spontaneity; that is to say, it cannot be regarded as belonging to mere sensibility. I call it *pure* apperception, in order to distinguish it from empirical; or primitive apperception, because it is a self-consciousness which, whilst it gives birth to the representation *I think*, must necessarily be capable of accompanying all our representations. It is in all acts of consciousness one and the same, and unaccompanied by it, no representation can exist *for me*. The unity of this apperception I call the transcendental unity of self-consciousness, in order to indicate the possibility of a priori cognition arising out of it. For the manifold representations which are given in an intuition would not all of them be my representations, if they did not belong to one self-consciousness, that is, as my representations (even although I am not conscious of them as such), they must conform to the condition under which alone they can exist together in a common self-consciousness, because otherwise they would not all without exception belong to me ".—" This universal identity of the apperception of the manifold given in intuition contains a synthesis of representations, and is possible only by means of the consciousness of this synthesis. For the empirical consciousness which accompanies different representations is in itself fragmentary and disunited, and without relation to the identity of the subject. This relation, then, does not exist because I accompany every representation with consciousness, but because I join one representation to another, and am conscious of the synthesis of them. Consequently, only because I can connect a variety of given representations in one consciousness, is it possible that I can represent to myself the identity of consciousness in these representations ; in other words, the analytical unity of apperception is

DEDUCTION OF THE CATEGORIES

possible only under the presupposition of a synthetical unity. The thought, 'These representations given in intuition, belong all of them to me', is accordingly just the same as, 'I unite them in one self-consciousness, or can at least so unite them'; and although this thought is not itself the consciousness of the synthesis of representations, it presupposes the possibility of it; that is to say, for the reason alone, that I can comprehend the variety of my representations in one consciousness, do I call them my representations, for otherwise I must have as many coloured and various a self as are the representations of which I am conscious ".

This, then, is the Transcendental Unity of Apperception. Kant sometimes calls it the *Original, Objective* Unity of Apperception to distinguish it from empirical apperception, and we must now make clearer the difference between the two. It is *original* because it must logically precede every other factor in consciousness, its supreme synthesis alone making consciousness possible; whereas the empirical apperception, in which two ideas are united by association, is secondary and only made possible by prior combination on the part of the higher principle. It is *objective* because the union it brings about is a union in the objective world itself, and holds good for the consciousness of every possible conscious subject; whilst the union in the empirical apperception is merely association of objects already phenomenal by a self that is also phenomenal, and therefore contingent and only valid for an individual consciousness. To be more explicit, the Transcendental Unity of Apperception (as revealed in the " I think ") is the first condition of all knowledge, whether of the self as object or of other objects. It is a unity the categories in constituting knowledge logically presuppose, and therefore a unity that is manifested in the objective world ; for only in relation to it can the manifold of sense, as determined by the categories, constitute one unity of experience. In the perception of freezing water, for example, I apprehend the two states, liquid and solid, as bound together in a relation of time, and this connection is objective and valid for all minds. And again, in the judgment " This body is heavy ", the conception of body and weight are combined with each other by means of the unity of apperception in the synthesis of perception ; and the judgment, far from expressing the connection of two notions by association, asserts that they are bound together in the object—are bound together, that is to say, not by arbitrary perceptions, so that the one suggests the other by association, but by a law that determines the perception and is logically prior to it.

On the other hand, the empirical unity of apperception is quite different. Here we do not get a union appearing in the object itself and holding good for consciousness in general, but merely a subjective union by association of objects previously subjected to the Transcendental Unity of Apperception—a union, therefore, that is entirely contingent and valid only for individual consciousness. In this case the Ego in which the two presentations are combined is itself phenomenal (consisting simply in a synthesised series of impressions of inner sense determined in time); it is as much object as any external object, because it is only known as it affects the inner sense, which, as subject to the categories, must bring it into time. When, therefore, I think of an object A as associated with an object B, because the two have frequently gone together in experience, I am expressing a relation between myself as phenomenal object and other phenomenal objects, and such particular combination naturally only holds good for my individual consciousness, not for consciousness in general.

The Categories as the Means of Bringing Sense Perceptions Under the Unity of Apperception

This, then, is the Transcendental Unity of Apperception—Kant's principle that every element in knowledge must be so combined with the other elements as to make possible the consciousness of one unchanging self throughout all experience, and that this consciousness of self only exists because every element is so combined by the spontaneity or self activity of one supreme faculty of synthesis. The Unity of Apperception is the highest principle of the possibility of knowledge, and everything that enters the mind must be so united as to comply with it (for otherwise it would either split the self and bring about a break in consciousness, or would be *for me* " as good as nothing "). In Kant's words " The proposition that all the various elements of our empirical consciousness must be bound together in one self-consciousness is absolutely the first synthetic principle in all our thinking". " The mere idea ' I ', in reference to all other ideas, (the collective unity of which it renders possible) constitutes the transcendental consciousness ". On this unity of self-consciousness, therefore, we can take our stand, and from it we can reason backwards to all that is presupposed in it or is necessary to make it possible. We can, and indeed must, say that everything that is to be known by us can only be known in such a way as to make possible the consciousness of one self ; that nothing can enter the mind, nothing can become object for us, unless it comply with the unity of apperception. Whatever conditions, then, are implied in this ultimate consciousness of self all our ideas must fall under ; and even if we admit that perception must precede apperception, we can yet lay it down a priori that the former must comply with the latter, and whatever conditions the one requires the other must necessarily obey.

Very well, then ; it being established that everything that can enter the mind or exist *for me* must comply with the unity of self-consciousness, it becomes clear that the manifold of sense must so comply. Accordingly, though the data of sense are in their source independent of the mind, yet we can lay it down that before they can enter the mind or become part of *my* perception they " must so come into the mind and be apprehended by it as to agree with the unity of Apperception ". As previously stated, however, as merely receptive sense could never give unity. " Combination does not lie in the objects and cannot be borrowed from them through sense perception and so taken up into the passive understanding: it is a thing achieved by the activity of the understanding itself, as a faculty of a priori synthesis, which brings the manifold of given ideas under the unity of Apperception." Unity, in other words, means synthesis, a faculty of self activity on the part of the understanding, and it thus becomes clear that before the manifold of sense can become united into objects and be brought into one unity of experience, there must be certain modes of subsumption under which such manifold must come, and the question is: What are these modes of subsumption? What are the rules by which sense is united by the understanding and objective synthesis is brought about?

Kant's answer is that this faculty is the faculty of judgment. In judging we are affirming an objective unity of perceptions, a unity which is universally valid because derived from synthesising the manifold of sense in certain a priori ways; in fact, it is Kant's contention that the various judgments of formal logic are nothing more than various modes of bringing given conceptions under the objective unity of apperception, or of combining them by means of the unity of apperception in the synthesis of perceptions. "I have never," he writes, "been satisfied with the explanation of judgment given usually by Logicians, that it is the conception of a relation between two conceptions. I will not raise the objection that this explanation is defective, as adapted only to categorical, and not to hypothetical and disjunctive judgments (which latter express a relation not of conceptions but of judgments): though this oversight leads to much confusion in the treatment of Logic. But I must note that it tells us nothing definite about the relation in question. When, however, I investigate more accurately, the relation of the given elements of knowledge in a judgment, and distinguish them from relations of association, established by reproductive imagination—relations which have merely subjective validity—I find that a judgment is nothing but the mode in which we bring given conceptions to objective unity of apperception. And this is just what is implied in the use of the verb of existence as the copula. That verb, in fact, distinguishes the objective unity of given ideas from their subjective unity: for it indicates that they are related to the original apperception and its necessary unity, and that even where the judgment itself is empirical and therefore accidental. Thus, by the judgment: 'Bodies are heavy,' I do not mean to assert that the conceptions of body and weight are *necessarily combined* in the empirical perception of them. But

DEDUCTION OF THE CATEGORIES 113

what I do mean is, that they *are combined with each other by means of the necessary unity of apperception* in the synthesis of perceptions, i.e., that they are combined according to those principles of objective determination under which all our ideas must come, if knowledge is to be derived from them. Only by subsumption under such principles can the relation of two conceptions be made such that it admits of being expressed in a judgment, i.e., a relation that is *objectively* valid ; whereas a relation of conceptions determined by the laws of association, could have only *subjective* validity. For by principles of empirical association, I could only be enabled to say that, when I carry a body, I feel a pressure of weight—but not to say that it, the body, is heavy. For this would be equivalent to saying that these two conceptions are bound together in the object—i.e., altogether apart from the state of the subject ; and not merely that the subject has perceived them together, however often it may be."

From this it will be seen that judgment and objective synthesis are one and the same thing. In judging we are affirming an objective unity of perceptions. A judgment in which two notions are bound together does not merely assert a connection of them by association (a connection derived from accidental perceptions differing for individuals, and therefore only subjectively valid) ; - it asserts that they are bound together in the object, are bound, that is to say, not merely by means of association coming from perceptions we have made at different times, but by a rule that is prior to it and determines it; and for this reason the judgment is universally valid.

We have now shown that every thing, including the manifold of sense, must come under the unity of apperception, if it is to exist *for me*. Further, we have shown that objective synthesis and judgment are one and the same thing; that, in fact, the various judgments of formal logic are nothing more than the means of uniting the manifold of sense into objects and bringing them under the Unity of Apperception. But, as was previously explained, the judgments in the logical table are the categories; consequently, we have now proved the main thing we set out to, namely, that the categories have objective validity and are the means by which all experience is constituted according to certain laws.

But though the categories are the means of uniting the manifold of sense into objects by bringing them under the unity of apperception, it is to be noted that they have no use except in relation to the sensuously given manifold. In themselves the categories are mere functions of unity, forms empty until filled by sense; consequently, deprived of sense content, they would not give perceptive recognition of anything whatever. Their only use is as a means of synthesising the sensuous impressions in space and time, or the space and time intuitions by themselves. In so far

DEDUCTION OF THE CATEGORIES 115

as they are concerned with the latter, it is possible to fill the categories with content a priori, and this, an a priori knowledge of the form of objects, is what we have in mathematics. But it is science of form only; whether there is any object corresponding to this form we cannot tell without sense material, and accordingly the categories can give no knowledge except in relation to material supplied by the senses. In short, though making experience possible, they are empty and meaningless except in relation to experience, and consequently can never enable us to extend our knowledge beyond the world of phenomena.

THE UNION OF UNDERSTANDING AND SENSE

Though it is now clear that the manifold of sense must be subject to the categories, which by a process of a priori synthesis unite them into objects, we have not yet shown how this is possible; indeed, remembering the results of the Æsthetic, that sensibility gives us sense impressions arranged in space and time, it would be very difficult to see how the categories could influence sensibility at all. For how could the understanding synthesise what is already in space and time? how could definite time relations impose themselves on an independent time existing on its own account? Clearly, if the manifold of sense are to come under the Unity of Apperception and become part of a system in one space and one time, as was proved in the last section, this means that sensibility as the system by which the matter for consciousness is arranged in space and time must be in harmony with the categories; that both space and time, and objects in space and time, must in certain aspects be derived from the Unity of Apperception. In short, as far as necessary and universal knowledge is concerned, there must be complete harmony between conception and perception; and this, as we shall now see, is in fact Kant's meaning. Indeed, in an article answering his critics, we find Kant interpreting Leibniz's pre-established harmony in this identical fashion when referring to the relationship of body and soul. After agreeing that it cannot be denied that the soul and that " (to us altogether unknown) substratum of those phenomena which we call the body " are things quite different from each other, he goes on to say : " But these phenomena themselves, as modes of perception, which are determined by the subjective nature of the soul that perceives them, are mere ideas. And as they are mere ideas, we can easily suppose that between the sensibility through which they are presented, and the understanding which is only another faculty of the same subject, there is a community which is regulated a priori by certain laws. This harmony between the understanding and the sensibility (which makes possible for us an a priori knowledge of the laws of nature) the Critique has asserted on the ground that without it experience would have been impossible. For, if the objects of experience were not conformable, as regards their perception, to the conditions of our sensibility, and also, as regards the combination of their manifold, to the principles by which the understanding unites its objects in one consciousness, they could not be taken up into the unity of consciousness or form part of our experience: and that is only another way of saying that for us they would be nothing at all." And only on these grounds, he contends, can we explain "why a nature, of which we know nothing except through experience, should yet be found to agree with our understanding, just as if it had been purposely adapted to it."

Thus, in Kant's meaning the "pre-established harmony" implies more than a harmony of two independent faculties: it means that there is one principle at work in both conception and perception. It means that, as far as necessary and universal knowledge is concerned, the modes of perception must be determined by conception; that the supreme principle of apperception, operating through the categories, must determine perception as it does conception; and only so can we explain the consciousness of a connected objective world, i.e., a world of objects all bound together as parts of one space and parts of one time.

To be more exact, Kant is here concerned with how the categories can determine the manifold of sense; and the answer he gives is that, as the form of the inner sense and of all possible perception is time, the only way in which the categories can determine sense is by operating on the inner sense in the form of time, and thereby fixing a priori the manner in which the manifold of sense is put together in time. In effect, his theory amounts to this: that the transcendental unity of apperception determines the inner sense in accordance with the categories; the form of the inner sense, as of all possible perceptions, is time; hence the categories, by determining the inner sense, are thereby determining all perception, in that they are fixing the ways in which the manifold of sense is put together in time. The categories thus constitute the conditions of the possibility of experience, and it is not surprising, therefore, that our experience should constitute a systematic unity; for as the manifold of sense is arranged by the categories in relation to *one self* (or unity of apperception), so the world of objects it gives rise to is necessarily *one world*.

But the categories cannot determine the manifold of sense directly, Kant explains, for in themselves the categories are mere functions of unity, purely *intellectual* in their nature, and cannot be brought into contact with the *sensuous* manifold without an additional faculty of mind that unites the two heterogeneous elements, or at least serves to express the categories in such a form as to enable them to determine the data of sense. As we shall later see, the *synthesis intellectualis* is thus imperfect except so far as it forms the basis of the *figural* synthesis, or *synthesis speciosa*. This latter synthesis Kant calls the *transcendental synthesis of the imagination*,

DEDUCTION OF THE CATEGORIES 119

since it is only made possible by the productive imagination, which is thus the ultimate productive factor of knowledge enabling the mind to schematise its objects. The productive imagination (which must be distinguished from the reproductive imagination, proceeding according to the laws of empirical association) gives sensuous expression to the categories, and thus enables them to determine the sensuous manifold. It is sensuous in so far as it can be applied to the matter of sense, and so far participates in the nature of sense; it is intellectual in so far as, in determining such matter of sense, its synthesis is an exercise of the spontaneity of mind as given a priori by the category. In a word, the synthesis of the productive imagination is an "effect of understanding upon sense"; in all its operations it expresses the categories, and in putting together the manifold of sense, it thus proceeds on necessary and universal lines, thereby enabling the understanding to prescribe its laws to nature, or to constitute our experience in accordance with certain time relations determined a priori by the categories.

From the above it will be seen that the transcendental synthesis of the imagination is the expression of the Unity of Apperception through the categories, and thus the means of constituting our objective world as a systematic unity by bringing the sensuous manifold under certain laws and thereby relating them to one unchanging self. Indeed, it is evident that objects are put together in conformity with the unity of space and time; hence, just as the unity of space and time is the result of the reference of their manifold to one transcendental self, so the conformity of objects to this unity, can only be explained as the result of a similar reference. But since the manifold of perception cannot be brought into relation to this unity of self except through the categories, it follows that the categories as conditions a priori of the possibility of experience are conditions a priori of the possibility of objects of experience.

That the conformity of objective synthesis to the unity of space and time is equivalent to its conformity to the categories, Kant shows by the following instances:—" When, by apperception of the manifold of sense, i.e., by gathering it together in relation to the unity of self, I represent a house as an object, I presuppose the unity of space, and of all external sensuous perception; and I make, as it were, a drawing of its shape in conformity with this synthetic unity. But if I abstract from the form of space, I find the same synthetic unity in the understanding in the form of a category: the category, namely, which is involved in all combination of homogeneous parts in one perception, the category of *quantity.*" " Again, to take another example, when I perceive the freezing of water, I apprehend two states (of fluidity and solidity), as standing in a relation of time to each other. But I necessarily represent the manifold as synthetically united in time, which, as an inner perception, is the

DEDUCTION OF THE CATEGORIES 121

presupposition of all other perceptions; for, unless time itself were a definite succession, no determinate relation of sequence could be presented in perception. But, again, if I abstract from the form of time, and regard this synthetic unity simply as a condition under which the manifold of perception in general may be combined, I find it the category of causality; and it is by the application of this category to my sensibility that I determine the relations of all that happens in time. Hence the perception of such an event, and therefore the event itself as a possible object of perception, stands under the conception of the relation of cause and effect."

This concludes the Transcendental Deduction of the Categories. Summing up the results, it has been proved that objects as such can only be determined by the synthesis of their manifold in relation to the Transcendental Unity of Apperception. It has been proved, further, that the categories are the forms of synthesis that serve this purpose; that, though in themselves they are mere empty functions of unity and useless except as determinative of the manifold of sense, they are yet the means of giving objective unity to this manifold, and that it is through them, and through them alone, that our experience became a systematic unity, a connected system in one space and one time. Now what is connected by categories must, as we have shown, be objectively valid and hold good for all consciousness; consequently the categories, as the conditions under which the manifold of sense can alone be arranged and related to the transcendental self, are the necessary and universal conditions by which phenomena are objectively connected. If we call the combination of phenomena according to law *nature*, the categories are the conditions or laws of nature; by determining the ways in which the synthesis of imagination puts together the manifold of sense in time, they prescribe their forms to nature. Hence, if we get to understand the ways in which the productive imagination expresses the categories in the form of time, so as to enable them to determine the ways in which the manifold of sense is put together in time, we shall discover the laws under which nature must fall, or in other words, the metaphysical principles of natural science. And this, as presented in the Analytic of Principles, will constitute the subject matter of the next chapter.

CHAPTER IV

THE ANALYTIC OF PRINCIPLES

WE concluded the last chapter by stating that the categories were so expressed by the productive imagination as to enable them to determine a priori the manifold of sense, and thereby to prescribe their forms to nature. But how the productive imagination did this was not clearly shown, and we now proceed to consider : first, the exact manner in which each of the categories become so expressed as to determine sense, and, secondly, the principles they constitute, or make our world of experience fall under, when so expressed. The first problem is that of the Schematism of the Categories ; the second that of the Principles of the Pure Understanding.

Dealing first with the Schematism of the Categories, according to Kant pure concepts and sense percepts are heterogeneous in their natures, concepts being purely intellectual and percepts sensuous. How, then, are they united ? How do we subsume what is given in sense under the categories, or, in other words, apply the rules of the pure understanding to make judgments about our particular experiences ? Clearly there must be some mediating factor between the two, something which is pure (or a priori) and yet at the same time sensuous. This mediating factor Kant calls the *Transcendental Schema of the Understanding*, and its nature is to include both the a priori factors of the categories, on the one hand, and to bring under them the particular sense manifold, on the other. What have we that complies with these requirements? Kant answers *time*, for that alone is both pure and sensuous. All our experiences, we know, are ordered in time; they all occur at particular moments of time and endure throughout particular periods of time. Hence, if the understanding is to impose its categories on sense, connecting and relating sense material in certain universal ways, it can only do so by use of the time form. The question, How are the categories schematised? resolves itself, therefore, into: How can they be applied to the inner sense, and so through it be applied to the matter of all sense? If only we are able to translate each of the categories into time, it will be easy to see how all sense material can be subsumed under them.

Now just as the understanding constitutes the categories, so it is the productive imagination, Kant contends, that produces the transcendental schema, determining space and time by means of the categories. It need scarcely be said, however, that Kant does not use the word imagination in the ordinary sense of a faculty of artistic invention: he means the faculty by which general notions are used to determine something without our forming the image of it, i.e., the power by which I can relate the categories to the general conditions of space and time, and thus determine the rule under which a particular image would have to come if and when it is drawn. Thus, when I form the general idea of a triangle I am not thinking of any particular triangle, and have in fact no image in my mind; I am simply laying down the general rules under which all triangles must fall, or the method of procedure which my imagination must comply with in order to form an image of, or to draw, any particular triangle. And the same, in fact, applies to all general ideas; in schematising, we are, according to Kant, bringing the categories into relation with the general conditions of space and time, and are thereby determining the rule under which any particular image must come without actually producing it. It is this particular power of schematising the categories by the productive imagination that makes mathematics possible; when we schematise the categories of Quantity and Quality, we bring them into relation with the conditions of space and time, and without producing any image, yet determine a priori the laws of space and time under which all images must come. The schematism of the categories is the translation of them into the forms by which they can determine sense, and this is essential before they can have objective application and enable us to transform what is given in sense into our world of objects.

Since, then, the categories must be schematised before they can become applied to the material of sense, and since expression in time is the only means by which they can be so schematised, the question is: How can the categories coming under the heads of *Quantity*, *Quality*, *Relation*, and *Modality* be translated into time? What are the modes of time by which they can so affect sense as to give the ordered experience called nature?

Starting with *Quantity*, we have to recognise that all objects of outer sense are quanta, in so far as they are spatial, as likewise are all objects of the inner sense, in so far as they are temporal. In space and time, therefore, we have pure images of quanta—quanta respectively of the outer and inner sense. Now since even objects of the outer sense must as states of consciousness also come under the inner sense, this means that all objects whatever must necessarily be quanta of the inner sense, or in other words must be in time. But time, as we have seen, can only be produced by the synthesis of homogeneous units, which we call numbering. The schemata of *Quantity* is therefore *number* or time series; and taking the three categories under this heading, we find *singularity* can be expressed as one moment of time, *particularity* as several moments, and *universality* as a totality of moments.

Going on to *Quality*, the empirical element of feeling has here to be introduced. " Between reality (presentation of feeling) and zero, i.e., the complete emptiness of intuition in time, there is a difference which has a quantity. For between each given degree of light and darkness, between each degree of heat and complete coldness, each degree of weight and of absolute lightness, each degree of the containing of space and of totally empty space, progressively smaller degrees can be thought of, and similarly between consciousness and complete unconsciousness (psychological darkness) continually smaller degrees exist. Hence no perception is possible that would prove an absolute void; for instance, no psychological darkness that could be viewed otherwise than as a consciousness which is but surpassed by another stronger consciousness, and the same in all cases of feeling." The schemata of *Quality* thus becomes *time-content* or *degree*, and the three categories of *reality, limitation* and *negation*, are schematised as that of *filled, filling*, and *empty* time. This schemata of Quality provides the second application of mathematics to natural science (mathesis intensorum), just as the schemata of Quantity provided the first (mathesis extensorum)

The schematism of the categories coming under *Relation* is simpler. *Substance*, which as a pure concept is that which is always subject and never predicate, becomes schematised as *persistence of the real in time*, or that which remains permanent throughout all change. *Causality*, as a conception of the relation of reason and consequent, becomes schematised as invariable sequence, or *regular succession in time*. And *community*, or reciprocal causality of substances in respect of their accidents, becomes schematised as *invariable coexistence*, or "the simultaneous existence of the qualifications of the one substance with those of the other, according to a universal rule." These may be described as the time-determinations *change and continuance, succession*, and *simultaneity*, or summarised as representing *time-order*.

This completes the schematism of those categories that actually constitute experience; those under the heading of *modality* only express the relation of objects of conception to our faculty of cognition, or explain the use of the terms possible, actual, and necessary in the world of experience. The category of *possibility* is schematised as "agreement of the different elements gathered together in the conception of an object with the conditions of time in general" (i.e., that an object is possible simply means that there is nothing in the nature of time to prevent its existence). The category of *actuality* is schematised as *existence at a definite time;* and that of *necessity* as *existence at all times*. In other words, these categories expressed in time-determinations become *sometime, now, always;* and may be summarised as representing *time-complex*.

This, then, is the manner in which the purely intellectual categories are translated into time, and can become applied to the inner sense, and so through it to the matter of all sense. The categorised time-determinations may be summarised as representing the *time-series*, the *time-content*, the *time-order*, and the *time-complex;* and, as the matter of sense can only be known through these determinations, they are instrumental in giving us the ordered experience we call nature. If this be correct, it is evident that these time-determinations will furnish us with the various metaphysical principles of science—the schemata of *Quantity* and *Quality* supplying the principles of mathematical science, the subordinate schemata of *Relation* and *Modality* the dynamical principles ; and to these, as set out in the Principles of the Pure Understanding, we now turn.

THE PRINCIPLES OF THE PURE UNDERSTANDING

Since the categorised time-determinations furnish the metaphysical principles of science, it logically follows that these principles will become divided into four branches, corresponding to the four headings of Quantity, Quality, Relation and Modality. They are arranged by Kant under the following titles :—

Mathematical	*Dynamical*
1	3
Axiom of Intuition	Analogies of Experience
2	4
Anticipation of Perception	Postulates of Empirical Thought in General.

Of the mathematical principles, the schema of time-series or number (corresponding to Quantity) gives the Axiom of Intuition ; the scheme of time-content (corresponding to Quality) the Anticipation of Perception. Likewise in the dynamical principles, the schema of time-order (corresponding to the categories of substance, causality, and reciprocity) give the three Analogies of Experience ; and the schema of time-comprehension (corresponding to the categories of possibility, actuality, and necessity) the Postulates of Empirical Thought in General.

The two mathematical principles determine all phenomena as extensive and intensive quanta, and therefore justify the a priori application of mathematics to all experience ; indeed, they carry unconditional necessity, for we cannot imagine or perceive anything without them. But the remaining principles relate, not to the constitution of objects, but " to the existence of these objects in relation to each other, and to the understanding " ; and they therefore only carry *contingent* necessity, i.e. they are necessary only so far as experience brings them into play. Of these latter, the three Analogies of Experience (the laws of substance, causality, and reciprocity) are the principles according to which it is possible for objects of experience to be inter-related in that systematic unity which is disclosed to us in experience ; so that objects all have definite places in the context of experience, and action in one part necessarily presupposes action in another according to universal laws. The Postulates of Empirical Thought do not determine objects or their relationships, but simply express the relation of objects of conception to our faculty of cognition; in other words, they explain the use of the terms *possible, actual,* and *necessary,* in that they tell us the conditions any object of conception must comply with in order to fall under these three categories.

The above will give an idea of the general division of the principles, but, before going further, it is important to understand more clearly the distinction between the mathematical and dynamical principles. When speaking of the categories in the Metaphysical Deduction Kant, after distinguishing those of Quantity and Quality as mathematical and those of Relation and Modality as dynamical, said : the former " relate to the *objects* of perception, whether pure or empirical; the latter to the *existence* of the objects in relation to each other, and to the understanding." It must be understood that when, in this passage, Kant distinguishes " *objects* of perception, whether pure or empirical " from " the existence of these objects in relation to each other ", he has a very distinct meaning; and, as Caird shows in his " Philosophy of Kant ", the best way of realising this will be to grasp the great difference between representing objects to oneself in imagination, on the one hand, and actually determining them as existent, on the other. In the former case, i.e., in imagination, the only conditions I have to comply with are the conditions of space and time, and consistent with these I can picture all kinds of creations that could never hold good of experience ; but in the latter, there are other conditions to comply with in addition to those of space and time, for the unity of experience consists of a system of objects all in relation to each other, and to determine an object as existing, i.e. to actually know it, means to fix it in necessary relations to other objects. Thus, whilst I can easily imagine the most absurd creations provided only they do not fail to comply with the general conditions of space and time, if I come to try and *know* such ideas as existent, I shall find them impossibilities. For here I cannot take various ideas and piece them together quite arbitrarily, as in imagination; each part of the experience has to be in relation to other parts, or, otherwise expressed, there will be other categories used besides those of Quantity and Quality, and these categories will necessarily demand that one portion of experience should be in relation to the other. Thus, the distinction in question comes back to this: that I can imagine what I cannot know, because in imagination I abstract from the context of experience, being only restricted to the categories of Quantity and Quality (or the general conditions of space and time); whereas, in determining objects as existent, or in actual experience, I find myself tied down to other conditions additional to those of space and time. Here various of the dynamical categories come into operation, and before I can know any object it must stand in certain necessary relations to other objects, and the freedom I had in imagination is thus curtailed.

This distinction between the mathematical and dynamical principles, or between the different restrictions imposed on imagination and on the constitution of experience, is further brought home when Kant tells us the mathematical principles are principles of "a synthesis of homogeneous elements, which do not necessarily belong to each other"; whereas the dynamical principles are principles of the "synthesis of heterogeneous elements, which necessarily belong to each other." In other words, the mathematical principles, as principles of quantitive synthesis do not necessarily force me to go on or to stop at any particular number or degree. Here there is nothing to force me to combine the elements at all: all required is that if I do so, I must do so in a determinate way. But, on the other hand, the synthesis of heterogeneous elements means that the elements brought together in synthesis are complimentary to each other, and in the dynamical principles we are therefore compelled to go on combining for ever in an attempt to reach an absolute whole of experience.

From the above it is clear, then, what Kant means when he says that mathematical categories "relate to the objects of perception, whether pure or empirical"; the dynamical categories "to the *existence* of these objects in relation to each other and to the understanding". In effect, he is saying: the only purpose of the mathematical categories is to determine the conditions under which any object by itself, and independent of other objects, may be represented in space and time; therefore so long as you are only using the categories of Quantity and Quality, the question of relationship of objects to each other, or to the understanding, does not arise. But when, in addition, you come to use the dynamical categories, you are not only held down to the general conditions of space and time, but compelled to fix all your objects in necessary relations to each other in one context or systematic unity of experience. Here you will find that nothing can ever become existent, or a part of actual experience, unless it complies with the relations demanded by the context of experience as a whole; and in point of fact, the categories of Modality, concerned with the relation of objects of conception to the faculty of cognition, will tell you how far a conception is possible or otherwise in experience without your trying to determine it.

So much, then, for the difference between the mathematical and dynamical principles. The former are necessary to the construction of all experience; without them nothing can be known or imagined; and as *constitutive* principles of all knowledge, they naturally carry absolute necessity. But the latter " do not concern the existence of objects but only refer to *relation of existence*, and avail to contribute, consequently, only *regulative* principles. In their case, therefore, there will be no question of either *axioms* or *anticipations*. But *one* perception of sense in a certain relation of time to *another* being given us, they (these propositions) will authorize us a priori to say *how*, in said *modus* of time, the latter object or perception is necessarily connected with the former object or perception from the point of view of their existence mutually, but not *what*, from the point of view of extension or intension (quantity and quality) said latter perception actually is." These dynamical principles, therefore, only carry contingent necessity, for it is only in accordance with experience that they are brought into play.

The Mathematical Principles

Having grasped the general difference between the mathematical and dynamical principles, we can now proceed to deal with them both more fully. Starting with the mathematical principles—the " Axiom of Intuition " and the " Anticipation of Perception "—these determine all phenomena as extensive and intensive quanta, and therefore justify the application of mathematics to the concrete world. The principle of the Axiom of Intuition is that " all phenomena are, with reference to their perception, extensive quantities ". And this follows from what has been said of the nature of space and time. For it has been shown that space and time are necessarily represented as extensive quantities, i.e., they only exist by a continuous synthesis of homogeneous units. Further, it has been shown that it is only in space and time that all objects and events can have being ; hence it follows that their manifold must be put together in the same manner as the manifold of space and time are put together ; which is to say, that they, too, must be extensive quantities. Kant calls this the " Axiom of Intuition " because intuition is the term he used for the mode in which everything is given or perceived, and accordingly to say that " all phenomena are extensive quantities " is the same as saying " all intuitions are extensive quantities ", since all objects must be intuited in the same way. From this principle Kant held that atoms (entities not further divisible), about which so much was talked in the physics of his day, could never be objects of consciousness ; for, if everything given in consciousness must necessarily be extensive, it follows that it must also be infinitely divisible.

The principle of the Anticipation of Perception is that " in all phenomena the real, that which is the object of sensation, has intensive quantity ; that is, has a degree ". And by this Kant means that, though all sensation as such is only given a posteriori, yet by the very nature of our minds we can lay it down a priori that every colour, weight, heat, etc., between it and negation, will be capable of lesser degrees of intensity. Though we cannot foretell what specific intensity an object not yet perceived will have, when it comes to be perceived, yet it is possible to anticipate that it must have some or other certain specific degree (of colour, weight, heat, etc.). In other words, if we cannot anticipate the *content* of sensation, we can anticipate the *form*. For whatever the object of sensation may be, in any case it is perceived in time, and whatever exists in time is necessarily a quantity. But the quantity of sensation does not consist, like that of intuition, in adding together homogeneous parts, otherwise a sensation could only be represented in a temporal series or as an *extensive* quantity. Sensation is clearly not an extensive quantity, a number of parts beside one another; it is an *intensive* quantity, a number of parts bound together in intensive unity. This, Kant contends, is due to a particular form of a priori synthesis, namely the category of Quality, which as an essential to the constitution of knowledge, necessarily prescribes its form to all experience. Thus, by the very nature of mind we can anticipate all sensation given in perception to this extent; we can say that, whatever sensation be given, it will have intensive quality or degree; that every sensation, between it and negation, will always be capable of lesser degrees of intensity. Incidentally, it follows from this principle that a vacuum can never be an object of sensation; and empty space and empty time not being possible objects of experience, Kant contended that it was impossible to use them (as was often done in his day) for explanations in physics.

From the above it will be seen that both the Axiom of Intuition and the Anticipation of Perception relate to the determination of quantity as regards all objects of possible experience, and as all determination of quantity is mathematical, these fundamental principles explain the application of mathematics to experience. In other words, both principles are based on number; in the one case it is a number of parts outside one another, in the other a number of successive gradations of sensation; and in this way the factors of extensity and intensity both permit of mathematical determination.

The Dynamical Principles

Proceeding to the dynamical principles, we must recall what was said respecting the different restrictions imposed respectively on imagination and the determination of actual knowledge, or, in other words, the nature of the mathematical and dynamical categories. In the former case it was shown that we could abstract from experience and represent objects independent of the context of experience as a whole, but that in the latter case every object and event had to take its place in necessary relations to other objects and events, so that our experience was a systematic unity in which objects and events were all related to each other as parts of one space and parts of one time. Now on what does this systematic unity of objects and events depend? Kant answers that it depends on the dynamical principles we are now considering. It arises from the application of the three schematised categories of *substance, causality*, and *reciprocity*, which indirectly determine experience. These categories, whose schema may be summarised as representing time-order, give rise to three principles, or Analogies of Experience, as Kant calls them, fixing a priori the dynamical relations in our context of experience and carrying contingent necessity. First, the category of substance, which when schematised becomes that which remains permanent throughout all change or persistence of the real in time, gives rise to the principle of the permanence of substance—"*in all changes of phenomena the substance is permanent, and its quantum is neither increased nor diminished in nature.*" Second, the category of causality, which when schematised becomes invariable sequence or regular succession in time, gives rise to the principle of causality—"*all changes take place according to the law of connection between cause and effect.*" And, thirdly, the category of Reciprocity, which when schematised becomes invariable coexistence, or "the simultaneous existence of the qualifications of the one substance with those of the other, according to a universal rule", gives rise to the principle of co-existence—"*all substances, so far as they can be perceived as coexistent in space, are always affecting each other reciprocally*". These three Analogies of Experience are of the greatest importance to the Kantian philosophy; for it is in these principles and their proof that Kant gives his final and long worked out answer to Hume's denial of the necessary relationship of cause and effect, which had been greatly the cause of his entering upon the critical enquiry. Hume, it will be remembered, had maintained that the principle of causality is nothing more than a subjective habit of mind, due to repeated experience of identical sequences. He had stated that all we really observe in contemplating nature is succession and change; that, as far as the objects observed are concerned, there was in fact no difference between observed succession and causation; and he had contended that the so thought necessary connection which the mind forms of changes in the external world is nothing more than a habit our minds have formed from custom, due to continually seeing the same succession. Now Kant, in answering this scepticism of Hume, universalised the problem. By asking How is consciousness of a world of objects all related as parts of one space and one time possible? he extended it not only to the principle of causality, but also to the principles of substance and reciprocity; and the answer he arrived at is that it is only possible by reason of these principles being a priori conditions of consciousness. The principle of causality cannot have come from experience, because it is necessary to experience; consciousness of succession does not lead to causality, because without the principle of causality there could be no consciousness of succession. And likewise with the principles of substance and reciprocity. Repeated experience of the same perception or object cannot explain the conviction that there is in objects something, which, throughout all change, remains identical with itself and can neither increase nor diminish, because consciousness that an object or perception is the same in its recurrent appearance is only made possible by the principle of substance; and in the same way, repeated coexistence of objects in one space cannot have implanted in us the belief that they are reciprocally necessary to each other, since without the principle of reciprocity existed a priori in the mind, objects could never be determined as coexistent in one space. In short, Kant contends that the three principles of substance, causality, and reciprocity cannot have come from experience because they themselves are instrumental in constituting experience; and he proves all three, on the transcendental method, by showing that there could be no systematic unity of experience, no consciousness of a world of objects and events all related as parts of one space and one time, without these principles were a priori conditions of consciousness.

In giving a short explanation of Kant's proof of these three principles, we cannot do better than quote the epitome of the same given in Caird's " Philosophy of Kant ". First, as to *substance*, Caird says :—" Experience is a knowledge of objects, all whose successive phases are connected together as events in one time. If this unity of time, as that *in* which all changes occur, were not presupposed, there could be no idea of change at all. A consciousness of time, as something not itself changing, is the necessary correlate of a consciousness of change or succession *in* time. But time in itself cannot be an object of perception; nor is it a general idea given along with each perception; for then we should be able to date a perception in reference to absolute time, and that without relating it to any other perceptions. But, on the contrary, it is only as we connect a perception with other perceptions, that we can represent it as in time at all. Time, in other words, is a mere form given to the relations of perceptions, which presupposes that they are otherwise related. We can connect events as *in* time, only in so far as we relate them to each other in the same way that the moments of time are related, and there must, therefore, be some determination given to objects as *in* time, which corresponds with unity or self-identity of time itself. As all times are in one time, so all changes must be in one permanent object. The conception of the permanence of the objects is implied in all determination of its changes. 'Change involves, that one mode of existence follows another mode of existence in an object recognised as the same. Therefore a thing which changes, changes only in its states or accidents, not in its substance; and, to use an expression only apparently paradoxical, only the permanent changes, while that which has nothing abiding in it cannot suffer change.' An experience of absolute annihilation or creation—of an object coming into existence from nothing, or an object ceasing to be—is impossible; for it would be an experience of two events, so absolutely separated from each other, that they could not even be referred to one time ; in other words, they could not be regarded as belonging to one world of experience. And as it is on the synthesis of phenomena that the consciousness of the identity of self depends, there could not be one consciousness of self in a being that had two such experiences. We cannot, indeed, assert that the creation or annihilation of substance is an *impossibility*, but we must assert that it is an *impossible experience*. It is absurd, therefore, to explain the idea of substance as a result of the empirical consciousness of the similarity of successive or recurrent perceptions ; for the consciousness of such recurrence or continuity of perception already involves that these perceptions are determined in relation to a permanent identity."

Next, going on to Kant's contention that the a priori nature of causality can be proved by showing that any judgment of sequence presupposes the judgment of causality, Caird proceeds :— " Time is a mere form of the relation of things, and cannot be perceived by itself. Only when we have connected events with each other, can we think of them as in time. And this connexion must be such that the different elements of the manifold of the events are determined in relation to each other in the same way as the different moments in time are determined in relation to each other. But it is obvious that the moments of time are so determined in relation to each other, that we can only put them into one order, i.e., that we can proceed from the previous to the subsequent moment, but not vice versa. Now, if objects or events cannot be dated in relation to time, but only in relation to each other, it follows that they cannot be represented as in time at all, unless their manifold is combined in a synthesis which has an irreversible order ; or, in other words, unless they are so related according to a universal rule, that when one thing is posited, something else must necessarily be posited in consequence. In every representation of events as in time, this presupposition is implied ; and the denial of causality necessarily involves the denial of all succession in time."

The same argument applies to coexistence in space, and the principle of reciprocity. "We cannot," says Caird, "represent objects as coexisting, by a direct reference of them to space ; for space is not perceived by itself, and objects are perceived as in space only when they are related to each other, as the parts of space are related. The relation of spaces must therefore be perceived *in* objects, if these objects are to be perceived as *in* space. But the parts of space are necessarily represented as reciprocally determining each other. Hence, only in so far as phenomena are represented as reciprocally determining each other, can they be referred to objects in space. The same necessity, therefore, with which each space is represented as determined by all other spaces, must be found in the relations of objects, for only as it is found in

THE ANALYTIC OF PRINCIPLES

the relations of objects, can it be found in the relations of the spaces which they occupy."

THE POSTULATES OF EMPIRICAL THOUGHT

Dealing, finally, with the Postulates of Empirical Thought, these are of less importance than the other classes of synthetical principles. They do not in the least constitute experience, in the sense of determining objects or their relationships, but simply express the relation of objects of conception to our faculty of cognition; that is to say, they explain the use of the terms *possible, actual* and *necessary*, in that they lay down the conditions any object of conception must comply with in order to fall within these categories. Thus, we can say :—(1) " That is *possible* which agrees with the formal conditions of experience (both of perception and conception) " ; (2) " That is *actual*, which is connected with the material conditions of experience " ; and (3) " That is *necessary* (or exists necessarily), the connection of which with actuality is determined in accordance with the universal conditions of experience ".

We will deal with each of these separately. As far as the first postulate is concerned, it is clear that any conception that agrees with the conditions of perception and conception must be possible; for these are the conditions of all experience, and any conception complying with them has nothing to prevent it being a possible experience, however lacking the evidence as to its actual existence. But, on the other hand, before we can say that anything is actual or real it must (as the second postulate lays down) be connected with the material conditions of experience; that is to say, we must either have sensible perception of it, or, at least, know that it is connected, according to the Analogies of Experience, with something else already sensibly perceived. Thus, though, as far as this latter point is concerned, we may have no sensible experience of a certain thing, because, say, our senses are not capable of being so adjusted as to perceive it, yet we can say it must exist if it follows, according to the Analogies, from something we have perceived; but in all cases the sensible perception of something from which to form the inference must be first given, and in no case can we speak of the actuality of the thing otherwise. The third postulate—"That is necessary (or exists necessarily), the connection of which with actuality is determined in accordance with the universal conditions of experience"—is really only a repetition of the inference of actuality that can be formed under the second postulate; namely, that, given sensible perception of a certain thing, we can, in accordance with the Analogies of Experience, necessarily infer the existence of another. The postulate lays down the rule that only that which follows, in accordance with the Analogies of Experience, from something already perceived can exist necessarily. Hence that nothing can be known to exist purely a priori, but that the highest necessity that can ever be

THE ANALYTIC OF PRINCIPLES 147

found is only that a thing can be known relatively a priori; or, as Kant expresses it, "necessity of existence can be cognised, never from notions, but only from the connexion, according to general laws of experience, with that which has already been perceived."

This, then, concludes the metaphysical principles of science. The first two principles determine things as *quantities*, and are therefore *mathematical;* the remainder determine the *existence* of things—the Analogies of Experience in relation to each other, the Postulates of Empirical Thought in relation to our faculty of knowledge—and are therefore dynamical. Under these four headings, it may be said that Kant is simply marking off the boundaries of human experience and answering one of his initial questions: How is physical science possible? He is simply telling us how mind prescribes its forms to nature or the world as we know it, and how it is that nature therefore consists of necessary and universal principles. The principles he has laid down are assumed in the science of applied mathematics and in dynamical science. The application of pure geometry to the world of experience assumes that all phenomena are extensive quantities, and physics assumes that intensive magnitude can be given to the qualities of objects. Similarly, in all scientific determination of change the three Analogies of Experience are assumed: the permanence of mass, the necessary connection of things in time, and the reciprocal interdependence of things existing at the same time. Since these principles are never proved by science, but always taken for granted in all scientific investigation, the metaphysician naturally asks, " On what does their validity rest ? " Kant is simply telling us that their validity rests on our a priori forms of consciousness, that mind prescribes its forms to nature, and that *as modes of the necessary connection of phenomena* the principles must always hold good of our world of experience because we ourselves create that world out of the unknowable world of things in themselves.

This being so, we are now in a position to say that Hume and the Empiricists were wrong in denying validity to knowledge. Since mind prescribes its forms to nature, we know a priori the universal forms of nature. We can say with apodeictic certainty that the phenomenal or perceived world will always be connected in certain intelligible ways, that our experience will always be of spatial and temporal things in fixed order, of things necessarily related as substance and accident, cause and effect, and as reciprocally influencing one another ; for this is the *necessary* element in phenomena supplied by the mind. But the *content* of phenomena, what particular sensations, colours, sounds, weights and so forth will be given, we cannot predicate a priori; for this we have naturally to go to experience, to the *matter* of knowledge. All we can say a priori is that, whatever the given matter may be, the mind will

THE ANALYTIC OF PRINCIPLES 149

organise and arrange it according to its a priori rules, and that these rules as modes of connection of phenomena will therefore carry necessity and universality throughout the whole of nature or the world when known.

Conclusions of the Analytic

The Division of the World into Noumena and Phenomena

In the opening chapter it was explained how Kant's object was to limit the scepticism of Hume, on the one hand, and the " dogmatic " metaphysics of the Wolff-Leibniz school, on the other ; and having now completed the positive side of his theory of knowledge, we are in a position to see how far he succeeded in this, and to understand how the new theory of knowledge, though by no means a compromise of two old theories, yet retained the best features of both. First, as far as Hume's scepticism is concerned, it is clear that on Kantian principles the Scottish philosopher was wrong in denying validity to knowledge of matters of fact, in the sense of doubting the necessity and universality of the main principles of physics. Since mind prescribes its forms to nature, we know a priori the universal forms of nature ; and though it is true, as Hume insisted, that all knowledge is experience, and as far as the *content* or *matter* of knowledge is concerned science is never relieved of empirical observation, yet we can say a priori that, whatever *matter* may be given, the mind will always arrange it according to its a priori rules, and that these rules as *modes of connection of phenomena* will always carry necessity throughout the whole of nature. Mathematics carries necessity and universality because all phenomena must fall within the a priori space and time forms, which are conditions of all consciousness; natural science carries necessity and universality because its principles rest on the categories, and the categories prescribe their forms to nature. Assuming the validity of Kantian principles, we can thus say with apodeictic certainty that the phenomenal or perceived world will always be connected in certain intelligible ways; that our experience will always be of spatial and temporal things in fixed order, of things necessarily related as substance and accident, cause and effect, and as reciprocally influencing one another. In a word, the principles which the scientist assumes as necessary working postulates have their validity firmly established; and in this respect Hume was wrong and Wolff and Leibniz were right. But here comes the fallacy of the latter school; though we have certain knowledge of these modes of connection of phenomena, we must remember that they are entirely restricted to phenomena. Of the supersensuous, of things and their relationships (if there be any such) outside the way they affect consciousness, we have no knowledge whatever; and in this respect, in his denial of all knowledge of the supersensuous, Hume was right, and Wolff and

Leibniz were wrong, in that they extended beyond experience notions only valid within experience. Our knowledge is not of things in themselves, nor is it the knowledge of the relationships of things-in-themselves; it is knowledge of phenomena, knowledge of transcendental objects as perceived and connected by the mind, and since such modes of perception and connection are entirely a priori, they must on no account be applied to things in themselves.

This, in brief, describes Kant's position in relation to Hume and the Wolff-Leibniz school, or, more generally, in relation to Empiricism, on the one hand, and Rationalism, on the other; and the position is such that it is scarcely surprising that by many critics the new philosophy should have regarded it as a mere repetition of old theories. On the one side, it states *all knowledge is experience*—a conviction held by Bacon, Hume, Locke, and the English Empiricists; on the other, *all knowledge is only possible through a priori concepts*—a theory insisted on by Descartes, Spinoza, and Leibniz. Was it not natural that adherents to these two schools should catch at one side of this double theory, the one party holding Kant to be nothing more than an Empiricist and the other looking upon him as just an old-fashioned idealist? And again, is it to be wondered at that others who escaped these errors, should yet have regarded Kant as a mere reconciler of two old conflicting theories? But even from a brief exposition like the foregoing it will be clear on what gross misunderstanding such criticism rests. It is true that his theory states *all knowledge is experience,* and it is true again that it states *all knowledge is possible only by concepts not obtained from experience;* but neither is the complete truth. The complete truth states that *all knowledge is experience, but this experience as such is only possible by pure concepts.* Or turning the statement round, we may say that, though experience as such is possible only by pure concepts, yet these pure concepts make experience possible only in so far as they are brought into relation with the manifold of sense; and neither of these factors taken alone can possibly give knowledge.

In the Analytic Kant, as we have seen, completed his exposition of the conditions that make knowledge possible; and having arrived at this stage, it is only natural that, before finishing this section, the question of the nature of knowledge should pass into the question of the limits of knowledge. Now from what has been said on the first question, it is clear that our knowledge is only knowledge of things as they appear in perception, and since the process of perception completely transfigures them by reason of its a priori forms of sense and understanding, it follows that sensuous knowledge can in no wise give us knowledge of things in themselves. In holding this opinion Kant is not altogether by himself; many philosophers, even from the time of the ancients, had recognised that sensuous knowledge is far from being knowledge of things in themselves. But certain of these philosophers, though recognising that we cannot know things in themselves through sense, had yet held that we can think them (indeed, Wolff and Leibniz had even constructed a metaphysic on these lines); and to distinguish what was known in perception (the sensuous) from what was thought (the intelligible) they had called the one *phenomena* and the other *noumena*. Kant is now concerned with asking, How far and in what sense the conception of noumena is possible ? Whence, if at all, can such a conception arise ? In order to answer this question we must again pass through what we have found to be true of knowledge, and try and see if in any stage of the logical process of consciousness there is any ground for the idea.

Starting with perception, the Æsthetic showed that the perception of objects is only possible under the forms of space and time, which belong to the mind itself and not to the *matter* presented to the mind ; and to this the Analytic added the further condition that sensations could only be converted into objects by means of the categories, which are again a priori. Thus, from what has been found true here it is clear that knowledge of noumena, if we have it, certainly does not arise from perception. But if perception fails us, what of the understanding with its categories ? Can this give us the idea of noumena ? Again, the answer must be in the negative. Apart from their relation to sense, the categories are mere functions of unity, and in themselvss do not enable us to determine any objects as such. Hence we are finally driven to ask the same question of the unity of apperception. But here again we are disappointed; for the unity we have in self consciousness is not knowledge of any thing, but only the unity of the manifold of sense in relation to the unity of the ego that apprehends it, and even this is only made possible by the application of the categories to the matter of sense.

Thus, neither in sense, understanding, nor unity of apperception have we any positive ground for forming the idea of noumena. But for all that Kant urges that the idea is not an unjustifiable one; for there are two senses in which the word noumenon can be used—a positive and a negative sense. In the positive sense a noumenon would be an object known non-sensuously, i.e., an object given in intellectual intuition; in the negative sense it would simply be the conception of an object not given in sensuous perception, or in other words, simply the thought that the thing in itself is an object that can never be given in sense. As far as the first sense is concerned, a noumenon is for us quite impossible; for the human understanding is discursive, not intuitive. But a noumenon in the negative or limiting sense, that is to say, as a concept that simply marks the boundaries of sensibility, is not only quite permissible, Kant contends, but is forced on us by the criticism of our

THE ANALYTIC OF PRINCIPLES 155

powers of perception and understanding. By such criticism we are enabled, indeed compelled, to say to sensibility: "You only apply to phenomena; the knowledge you give me is not of things in themselves but only knowledge of things as they appear under the a priori space and time perception and after being worked on by the categories, and beyond that you cannot go." And in so limiting the sphere of sensibility we set before ourselves the idea of a thing in itself, which as a transcendental object is necessary to the explanation of knowledge, even though we cannot think of it as quantity or reality, or as substance or any other of the human conceptions. If we call it a noumenon, it is only as the name given an unknown X, which we desire to show cannot be represented sensuously, and which is therefore so different from all phenomena, that we cannot even say whether it is within us or without us.

In Kant's own words, "The conception of a noumenon, i.e., of a thing which is to be thought not as an object of sense, but as a thing in itself (the object of understanding only) is not self-contradictory; for we cannot say that sense is the only possible mode of perception. Nay, this conception is even *necessary* to prevent us from extending sensuous perception to things in themselves, and so to limit the objective validity of the knowledge derived from sense. We give the name of noumena to all objects, just for the purpose of showing that such knowledge is not all that understanding can think. Yet in the end we have to acknowledge, that we cannot understand even the possibility of such noumena, and that the sphere of knowledge which we thus reserve beyond the region of phenomena, is for us quite empty." In this way, "understanding limits the sensibility without extending its own sphere. It warns us not to speak of things in themselves, but only of phenomena; and, in so doing, it sets before itself a thing in itself, but only as a transcendental object, which is the cause of phenomena, and not itself a phenomenon, and which, therefore, can be thought neither as quantity nor as reality, nor as substance, etc. (because all these conceptions require sensuous forms, in which alone they determine objects for us). Of this transcendental object we are unable to say whether it is in ourselves or out of us, whether it would be annihilated by our sensibility, or would continue to exist even if we no longer perceived it. If we choose to call it a noumenon, in order to show that we do not represent it as sensuous, we are at liberty to do so. But, as we cannot apply to it any one of the categories, the conception of it is for us empty and meaningless, except in so far as it calls our attention to the limits of our sensuous experience, by marking off a vacant space which we cannot fill up by the aid, either of possible experience, or of the pure understanding."

The above really represents Kant's final position in relation to the idea of noumena, but, as is well known, much controversy has centred round the point, a number of critics holding that the idea of the thing in itself is not consistent with Kant's theory of knowledge. In this book no pretence will be made to defend the philosopher's position in the controversy. It is, however, worth while mentioning that some at least of his critics have based their arguments on a most clumsy misconception of his meaning. The truth is that, after the publication of the first edition of the Critique, Kant was so often interpreted as an idealist and classed with Berkeley, that in the second edition he determined to make his position clearer, and to the *Postulates of Empirical Thinking* he appended a passage entitled "Refutation of Idealism," in which he endeavoured to prove more emphatically the existence of the thing in itself. The section was mainly directed against Descartes and Berkeley, the former of whom had contended that internal experience was immediate and therefore more certain than external; and in effect Kant's argument amounts to this : that we could not annihilate the idea of noumena or things in themselves or hold that internal experience was more real than external, because in truth internal experience, far from being more real than external, was in fact only made possible by the latter. Several critics have apparently misinterpreted this passage; they have taken it to imply the existence of *external* things in themselves, and have accused Kant of the gross inconsistency of trying to establish noumena *in space*. But it is clear that this was never the great philosopher's meaning. As he himself says, his sole aim was "to prove that internal experience in general is only possible through external experience in general"; and his theory is that space (though only phenomenal) being at any rate as real as time, existence in both has equal reality. We are therefore just as much compelled to assume objects in space as we are to assume the ego in time, and in fact, more so, since the unity of self consciousness is only the correlate of the unity of the manifold given in sense, and we have no reason to think that the former would exist independent of the latter. In a word, both outer and inner experience are equally phenomenal, and it is thus just as necessary to assume a noumenon or transcendental object in the one case as the other, though our knowledge of such noumena is in each case nil.

Thus, despite all criticisms, Kant always held to the idea of noumena. Indeed, he held that without the limiting concept of noumena as the ground of phenomena we could not explain knowledge at all; that, though we could not apply a single positive human conception to it, being unable even to regard it as permanent or to say whether it was within us or without us, yet as a negative concept limiting the boundary of sense it was absolutely essential. Thus, the bare trees of the winter will bring forth their leaves in the spring, the living body of to-day may be dead to-morrow, and in each case the phenomenon has changed, and science will endeavour to give us the empirical causes of such change. But what the noumenon corresponding to the phenomenon is or has done we cannot say, for not a single form of our consciousness can be applied to it. Similarly my knowledge of myself, my own internal states, is not knowledge of myself as I am in myself: it is simply phenomenal knowledge, knowledge of how I appear to myself after passing through the glass of consciousness; and though with internal knowledge, as with external knowledge, we are compelled to assume a noumenon or transcendental object, yet in the former case as in the latter we can say nothing about it. It thus follows from this theory that the real nature of the soul as of objects is quite unknowable, and, as we shall see when we come to deal with Rational Psychology, Kant, whilst repudiating all theoretical proofs of immortality, by the nature of his theory of knowledge, is logically compelled to leave the question open, contenting himself by simply rejecting all logical or purely intellectual arguments either for or against.

PART III

TRANSCENDENTAL DIALECTIC, OR THE DOCTRINE OF PURE IDEAS

CHAPTER I

THE IDEAS OF PURE REASON

Rational Psychology and its Paralogisms

IN the last chapter we completed the positive side of Kant's work, showing how in his answers to the two questions, How is pure mathematics possible? and How is pure science of Nature possible? he supported the absolute validity of the principles of science. We have now to turn to the more negative part of the Critique, and to examine his answer to the third question, How is metaphysics possible?—if not as a science, at least as a natural disposition of the mind.

Now from what was said in the conclusion of the last chapter, when we dealt with Kant's division of the world in Phenomena and Noumena, it is clear that the only answer to the question is that metaphysics as a science is most certainly not possible. All our knowledge is of phenomena only, and though there must be noumena "behind" phenomena as its grounds, we can know nothing of it, for not a single conception of our minds can be applied to it. Accordingly, as the problems of metaphysics—God, freedom, and immortality, as Kant conceived them to be—relate entirely to noumena and not phenomena, our knowledge of such matters would appear to be nil, being restricted to the phenomenal side of the boundary, so to speak.

But whatever be the case against metaphysics as a science, if there is one thing clearer than another it is that throughout the ages the mind of man has never been content to rest within the bounds of experience. It persists in passing into a higher region, a region, Kant contends, which, if it cannot know, it will endeavour to create for itself, by forming ideas of the unconditioned, and then reasoning about these as though they were objects of experience. Metaphysics, in a word, is a natural and ineradicable disposition of the human mind. After a Critical enquiry into the powers of reason, we may come to know its limits much as we come to know that the earth is going round the sun and not vice versa ; but we can never actually rid ourselves of the illusions it gives rise to, any more than we can cease to talk of the sun rising when scientifically we know much better. We have to understand, then, why it is that mind ever seeks to pass beyond experience—why it not only constitutes experience according to certain laws, but continually seeks to bring the conditioned under higher and higher conditions, until finally it imagines it has reached the condition which is itself unconditioned.

The matter is dealt with in the third division of the Critique, called the Transcendental Dialectic; and just as the two previous divisions were concerned with the question, How is experience possible? so this one deals with the question, How is dogmatic metaphysics possible? how is the mind constituted that it not only constitutes experience, but seeks to pass beyond it? We are here concerned with Pure Reason, or a faculty of Ideas, as opposed to Pure Perception and Pure Conception, whose analysis comprised the first two divisions of the Critique, and Kant draws a sharp distinction between these different faculties. Perception and Conception are entirely concerned with the constitution of experience out of the unknowable things-in-themselves, but, says Kant, if our minds consisted of sensibility and understanding only, we should be without any impulse to pass beyond what is given in phenomena as in fact we do. For this a further faculty is needed, namely Reason; and Kant is now concerned with investigating the nature of this faculty, showing it to be the basis of our forming Ideas of the unconditioned, and deciding, finally, whether these Ideas, unavoidable and necessary as problems to be solved, are to be regarded as giving knowledge of objects corresponding to them, or, on the contrary, are only regulative ideas necessary for giving systematic unity to our

THE IDEAS OF PURE REASON

knowledge and experience but incapable of extending knowledge beyond experience. As we shall see, Kant decides such Ideas are only valid in the latter sense. Though Reason by its very nature must form Ideas of the unconditioned, which are therefore quite valid as problems to be solved (and in a sense presupposed in all our knowledge and experience), he shows that their real purpose is to aid us in the investigation and arrangement of our knowledge and experience, and denies to them any value as giving knowledge of the metaphysical objects they promise. On the contrary, he shows that when, by the aid of the Idea of the unconditioned, we try to extend our knowledge beyond experience and regard these ideas as constitutive of real objects, or as giving knowledge of the Nature of the Soul, the Totality of the Universe, or the Being of All Beings, we are always engaging in some form of sophistical reasoning. The whole process is Dialectical or a logic of false show, and in Transcendental Dialectic Kant is engaged in exposing its errors, showing that, though the Ideas are valid as problems to be solved and produce an irresistible illusion of having extended our knowledge, they are really Ideas and nothing more, and by no possible means can our knowledge come up to them.

First, however, we must understand Kant's theory of the nature of Reason. Here Kant again takes his guide from ordinary Logic. Just as in the Analytic he found the key to the Categories and the Principles of the Understanding in those parts of formal logic dealing respectively with apprehension and judgment, so he now seeks the solution of his problem in that part of ordinary logic known as the syllogisms of Reason. These refer to the process of judging in accordance with rules, or the connecting of two judgments so as to obtain a third from them by necessary consequence, and are called syllogisms of reason in opposition to the syllogisms of the understanding, which draw one judgment from another immediately (without intervention of a third judgment); and Kant now takes the difference between these two as means of distinguishing the two faculties of Understanding and Reason. Commenting on the two classes of syllogisms, Kant says: " In every reasoning or syllogism, there is a fundamental proposition, afterwards a second drawn from it, and finally the conclusion, which connects the truth in the first with the truth in the second—and that infallibly. If the judgment concluded is so contained in the first proposition that it can be deduced from it without the mediation of a third notion, the conclusion is called immediate: I prefer the term conclusion of the understanding. But if, in addition to the fundamental cognition, a second judgment is necessary for the production of the conclusion, it is called a conclusion of the reason. In the proposition, *All men are mortal*, are contained the propositions, *Some men are mortal, Nothing that is not mortal is man*, and these are therefore immediate conclusions from the first. On the other hand, the proposition, *All the learned are mortal*, is not contained in the main proposition (for the conception of a learned man does not occur in it), and it can be deduced from the main proposition only by means of a mediating judgment. In every syllogism I first cogitate a rule (the major) by means of the understanding. In the next place I subsume a cognition under the condition of the rule (and this is the minor) by means of the judgment. And finally I determine my cognition by means of the predicate of the rule (this is the conclusion), consequently, I determine it a priori by means of reason. The relations, therefore, which the major proposition, as the rule, represents between a cognition and its condition, constitute the different kinds of syllogisms. These are just threefold—analogously with all judgments, in so far as they differ in the mode of expressing the relation of a cognition in the understanding—namely, categorical, hypothetical and disjunctive.* When, as often happens, the conclusion is a judgment which may follow from other given judgments, through which a perfectly different object is cogitated, I endeavour to discover in the understanding whether the assertion in this conclusion does not stand

* Examples of these three forms of syllogism :—
(1) *Categorical*, e.g., All things green are coloured ; this object is green ; therefore, it is coloured.
(2) *Hypothetical :* If a thing is green, it is coloured ; this object is green ; therefore, it is coloured.
(3) Disjunctive : A thing is not both green and yellow ; this thing is green ; therefore, it is not yellow.

under certain conditions according to a general rule. If I find such a condition, and if the object mentioned in the conclusion can be subsumed under the given condition, then this conclusion follows from a rule which is also valid for other objects of cognition. From this we see that Reason endeavours to subject the great variety of the cognitions of the understanding to the smallest possible number of principles (general conditions), and thus to produce in it the highest unity."

Thus, Kant concludes that the endeavour of Reason is always to find a principle to explain the combination of our thought, and it can never be satisfied until it has found a first principle. Reason must, therefore, be regarded as the faculty of principles, or rather the faculty that gives unity to knowledge by means of principles. Just as the function of the understanding is to combine the manifold of sense by means of its rules, so the function of Reason is to combine the rules of the understanding by bringing them under principles. It sets before the understanding an ideal of completeness and unity, which the understanding by itself could never possibly furnish; for, as we have seen, understanding only determines phenomena in relation to each other—it is entirely knowledge of conditioned experience—and if, therefore, Reason seeks, as it does, to complete the series of conditions, it follows that it must be quite an additional faculty. Reason, it is true, does not prescribe any law to objects in the sense of containing any ground

THE IDEAS OF PURE REASON 167

of the possibility of cognising or determining them as such ; but it constitutes a subjective law for the arrangement of the content of the understanding, and is therefore to be regarded as a transcendent synthesis, in that, though it is never found in phenomena or realised in sensuous experience, it is yet the mediate means by which we give systematic unity to phenomena by reducing the conceptions of the understanding to the smallest possible number.

Now this aim of unity and universality to which Reason points is nothing less than the unconditioned. For Reason has as its object the absolute totality in the synthesis of conditions ; by its very nature it ascends from the particular to the universal, from the conditioned to its conditions, and its ultimate object must necessarily be the unconditioned. Thus, whilst the unconditioned can never be given in experience (experience by its very nature being conditioned), it is the goal which Reason endeavours to reach. Where the conditioned is given, there Reason supplies out of itself the whole series of conditions, and the unconditioned is therefore a necessary object of pure thought. Kant calls such object of pure thought an Idea of Pure Reason, or a Transcendental Idea, in that it is a rational unity or product Reason supplies out of itself, no object ever being found to correspond to it in the world of sense. And as we shall see, in the Dialectic he is concerned with showing that, though the unconditioned as Idea or as a necessary problem of Reason is perfectly valid, it is a fallacy to infer, as had been done by certain metaphysicians of his time, that this Idea has extended our knowledge in the sense of having established it as referring to any existent object beyond experience. In other words, to argue : if the conditioned is given, the unconditioned is given as *Idea*, is true ; but to argue : if the conditioned is given, the unconditioned is given *as existence or object*, is false. In the first case we have a true syllogism ; in the second a dialectical syllogism. In the first we argue : given conditioned existence as a phenomenon, the unconditioned is given *as Idea ;* and this is a correct argument, but unfortunately one that denies the possibility of metaphysics. In the second case we consider the concept of the conditioned independent of our representation, regarding it not as phenomena but as referring to things in general, and, as Fischer expresses it, we argue : " *If the conditioned* (as things *per se*) *be given, the unconditioned is also given. But the conditioned is given* (merely as phenomenon). *Therefore the unconditioned is also given.*" The latter argument is thus dialectical. The concept of the conditioned, which is the middle term of the syllogism, is used in two different senses—in the major premiss as the thing in general, in the minor merely as phenomenon, and no conclusion is therefore possible. In this way Kant claims to have shown all metaphysic of the supersensuous to be based upon dialectical syllogisms. Whilst it is perfectly true to say that, if the conditioned is given, the unconditioned is given *as Idea* or as a necessary problem of reason, we must always remember that we can never solve the problem, since experience can never be adequate to the Idea, nor can the Idea be taken as giving knowledge of any object beyond experience.

From the above, then, we see that, wherever conditioned existence is given, the aim of Reason is to conclude from it the unconditioned—an ideal, it is true, that experience can never realise, but perfectly justifiable as Idea. Now conditioned existence is given us in three ways: as internal phenomena (existence within us), as external phenomena (existence without us), and as all possible experience or all objects of thought in general. Thus, by syllogism we may prove the idea of an unconditioned within us, of an unconditioned without us, and of an unconditioned in relation to all possible being. Otherwise expressed, Reason, in pursuing its ideal of the unconditioned in relation to these three different forms of conditioned existence, forms three different classes of Transcendental Ideas—the unconditioned unity of the thinking subject, the unconditioned unity of the series of conditions of a phenomenon, and the unconditioned unity of the condition of all objects of thought in general; these being the respective results of following the regressive movement of Reason according to the categorical, hypothetical and disjunctive forms of syllogism. Now the unconditioned unity of the thinking subject is the Idea of the Soul; the unconditioned unity of the series of the conditions of a phenomenon is the absolute constitution of the world-order, or the Idea of the Universe; and the unconditioned unity of the conditions of all objects of thought in general, the being of all beings, is the Idea of God. In Kant's words, "Transcendental Ideas arrange themselves in three classes, the first of which contains the absolute (unconditioned) unity of the thinking subject, the second, the absolute unity of the series of the conditions of a phenomenon, the third the absolute unity of the condition of all objects of thought in general. The thinking subject is the object-matter of Psychology; the sum total of all phenomena (the world) is the object-matter of Cosmology; and the thing which contains the highest condition of the possibility of all that is cogitable (the being of all beings) is the object-matter of all Theology. Thus pure reason presents us with the idea of a transcendental doctrine of the soul (Rational Psychology), of a transcendental science of the world (Rational Cosmology), and finally of a transcendental doctrine of God (Rational Theology)."

Now these three Ideas, as problems to be solved, are not fictions, but Ideas which Reason by its very nature presents to itself. The questions they raise are forced on us, in short, by the natural exercise of our rational powers; and we are thus compelled to ask, whether there really exist such unconditioned

THE IDEAS OF PURE REASON

objects, or whether, on the other hand, the proper use of Reason in seeking such unconditioned objects does not lie " in giving such direction to the understanding as may enable it at once to extend its researches to the utmost, and maintain the greatest unity and harmony with itself." In other words, the question of the Dialectic, which we are now about to enter on, is whether the alleged sciences of Rational Psychology, Rational Cosmology, and Rational Theology can enable us to determine the nature of the soul, the world, and God, or whether when, led on by the idea of the unconditioned, we form conceptions of such objects, we are not guilty of forms of sophistical reasoning. As already suggested, Kant's answer is that we are so guilty. Generally described the sophistry amounts to this : that taking an idea which is valid only in relation to experience, we separate it from this its experiential validity and regard it as itself determining an object of thought ; and the three branches of the Dialectic are concerned with an exposure of special peculiarities of this error. " There are three kinds of dialectical syllogisms of reason," says Kant, " as there are three ideas of reason, to which as conclusions, these syllogisms bring us. In the syllogism of the first class, I argue from the transcendental conception of the subject " (the Transcendental Ego) " in which there is nothing of difference or multiplicity, to the absolute unity of the subject itself ; though of the subject in itself apart from its relation of experience, I have no conception whatever. This dialectical syllogism I shall call the transcendental *Paralogism*. In the second class of sophistical syllogism, I start with the transcendental conception of the absolute totality of the series of conditions for a given phenomenon, and infer from it the unconditioned synthetic unity of the series, and as, in this case, there are always two possible ways in which this unconditioncd unity may be determined, each of which involves a contradiction, I reason from the self-contradiction of one of these ways of conception to the truth of the other—not observing that the argument may be retorted with equal effect. The state of reason produced by these dialectical arguments, I shall call the *Antinomy* of pure reason. In the third class of sophistical syllogism, I reason from the totality of the conditions under which I think of objects as such, *after* they have been given to me in sense, to the absolute synthetic unity of all the conditions of the possibility of things in general. In other words, I reason from things which I do not and cannot know by means of the mere transcendental conception I have of them to a Being of All Beings, an ens entiam, whom I do not know, even in a transcendental conception, and of whose unconditioned necessity I can form no idea whatever. This dialectical syllogism I shall call the *Ideal* of Pure Reason."

The criticisms of these three arguments constitute the three branches of the Dialectic. To the first of these, namely the Paralogisms of

THE IDEAS OF PURE REASON 173

Rational Psychology, we proceed straightaway; Rational Cosmology and Rational Theology will be dealt with in separate chapters.

RATIONAL PSYCHOLOGY AND ITS PARALOGISMS

The first of the Ideas of pure reason is the rational conception of the soul as the absolute unity of the thinking self, and in this division of the Dialectic Kant is mainly concerned with showing that the Idea or unconditioned unity here formed is the product of a transcendent use of the categories. All the assertions by which Rational Psychology had tried to demonstrate the immortality of the soul are shown to be so many paralogisms, arising from an illegitimate application of the category of substance to the pure unity of self (the analytical " I am I ") for which all objects exist, and the true nature of the self is held to be unknowable. It is true, Kant states in effect, that all knowledge and experience imply the unity of the knowing subject—this is what is meant by the unity of apperception—but this unity only exists in relation to what it unites, or the object it stands in opposition to, and in no possible sense can it be regarded as an object of knowledge. In Rational Psychology, however, an attempt is made not only to think of this unity of self independent of what it unites, but as itself constituting an object of knowledge— i.e. something given in intuition to which the categories can be applied—and by means of the categorical syllogism this leads to the idea that the soul is a simple, self-identical, self-existent substance, and therefore immaterial, indestructible and immortal. The fallacy of the argument thus lies in treating the unity of the self as though it were an object of knowledge; it is forgotten that the unity of self (for which all objects are) is really a quite unknowable something *behind* the categories, and that if we apply the categories to it we are only revolving in a circle, since the categories necessarily presuppose it.

To be more explicit, the objective world is essentially an object for a thinking subject, as we have seen; we know it only as we combine the data of sense by means of the categories in relation to the self. In this relation it is certainly true that, in the consciousness of this pure unity for which all objects are (the analytical " I am I "), we have the ultimate condition that makes experience possible; but it must be remembered that the consciousness we have of this unity in the " I think " is not in any sense empirical knowledge of it. The " I " (the thing) which thinks " is simply a transcendental subject$=$X, which is known only through the thoughts which are its predicates, and of which, if it is separated from other things, we cannot have the smallest conception." This pure ego lies " *behind* " the categories, so to speak, and determines objects by them; hence in any attempt we make to know it, we are merely placing it " *in front* " of the categories and thus turning round in a continual circle, since we must always make use of it in order to make any judgment concerning it. In other words, in any attempt we make to know the pure self, we are simply trying to know as an object that which we must presuppose to know any object; or, as Kant puts it, "the subject of the categories cannot, by thinking them, attain a conception of itself as an object, for in order to think them, it must presuppose its own pure self consciousness, i.e., it must presuppose the very thing it would explain." Thus, the true nature of the self is quite unknowable.

But Rational Psychology failed to see this. It tried to know the self as though it could be made an object amongst other objects, and did not realise that it thereby only got a consciousness of self (as object) in relation to self (as subject), i.e. the "determinable" self as opposed to the "determining" self. The supposed science was based on a confusion between the transcendental subject and the empirical self, object of the inner sense (the object-matter of empirical psychology); and all its assertions were really so many paralogisms, arising from transferring to the latter the logical characteristics of the former, the middle term in its syllogisms being used in two different senses. In this way, what ultimately happened was that the universal conditions under which objects are thought were turned into universal predicates of thinking beings as objects; and thus Rational Psychologists stated :—

1. As the ego is the subject implied in all con-

sciousness, the soul is thinking or immaterial substance;

2. As the ego is the unity in relation to which all objects are combined, the soul is a simple substance, and so not liable to dissolution;

3. As the ego is conscious of itself remaining a unity through all changes of its perceptions and thoughts, the soul is a substance always identical with itself, or in other words a persôn;

4. As the ego is that in relation to which alone we can be conscious of objects as existing, the soul has an existence apart from other things, though able to enter into relation with the body.

And in this way the soul was determined as a simple, self-identical, self-existent substance; therefore immaterial, indestructible, and immortal.

As previously explained, however, all these statements are only the outcome of taking the universal conditions under which objects are thought and turning them into universal predicates of thinking beings as objects. In reality the pure (unknowable) unity of self is something "behind" the categories, and is only known in relation to what it unites; and in effect Kant's answers to the four assertions are as follows:—

1. It is true that the thinking "I" must in every act of thought be looked upon as subject, and not as a mere predicate of thought; but this does not mean that I am objectively an independent substance.

2. It is true that the "I" of apperception

denotes a logical simple subject—the analytical "I am I"; but this does not signify that the thinking I is a simple substance, which, indeed, would be a synthetical proposition.

3. It is true that the ego is conscious of itself as remaining a unity through all changes of its perceptions and thoughts; but from this (analytical) identity there does not follow the identity of a thinking substance existing amidst all change of states.

4. It is true that, as a thinking being, I can distinguish my existence from other things external to me, including my own body; but this does not signify that this consciousness of myself would remain if there were no things external to me, and that I could therefore continue to exist without a body.

All the assertions of Rational Psychology are so many paralogisms, arising from an illegitimate application of the category of substance to the consciousness which the thinking *I* has of itself in all it unites. The pure unity of apperception— the analytical "I am I"—that, as stated before lies "*behind*" the categories, is turned into an object "*before*" them. It is forgotten that "I cannot know that as an object which I must presuppose in order to know any object, and that the *determining self* (thought) is distinguished from the determinable self (the thinking subject) as knowledge from the object of it." The fact is, "through the I or He or It (the thing) which thinks, nothing is set before our consciousness except a transcendental subject=X, which is known only through the thoughts that are its predicates, and of which, if it is separated from other things, we cannot have the smallest conception. In attempting to grasp it, in fact, we turn round it in a continual circle, since we must always make use of it in order to make any judgment regarding it. Here, therefore, we are brought into an awkward pass, out of which there is no escape; because the consciousness in question is not an idea which marks out for us a particular object, but a form which attaches to all ideas in so far as they are referred to objects, i.e., in so far as anything is thought through them."

Thus, in the Kantian philosophy the real nature of the self is quite unknowable, and as far as immortality is concerned, all we can do is to reject all a priori arguments either for or against. But, as in the question of the existence of a Supreme Being, this negative attitude of thought has consolation; for the fact that theoretical reason is powerless in the matter leaves room for proof on other grounds, and if, as we shall later see, the moral law or practical reason demands it as a necessary postulate we shall have proof that the Idea of the soul has some reality corresponding to it, even though the nature of that reality is quite unknowable.

CHAPTER II

KANT'S CRITICISM OF RATIONAL COSMOLOGY

THE ANTINOMIES OF PURE REASON

IN the beginning of the last chapter we explained Kant's theory of the nature of Reason, showing that wherever conditioned existence is given Reason by its very nature seeks the entire chain of conditions and forms an Idea of the unconditioned, whereby alone the conditioned is possible. We showed, further, that conditioned existence is given us in three different ways—as internal phenomenon (existence within us), as external phenomenon (existence without us), and as possible existence, or all objects of thought in general; hence that by syllogism we could prove the idea of an unconditioned within us, of an unconditioned without us, and of an unconditioned in reference to all possible being. Now Kant's treatment of the first of these Ideas, the Idea of the unconditioned within us, was fully dealt with in the latter part of the last chapter. Here it was shown that, though Reason by its very nature must present to itself such an Idea in reference to our psychological states, it was yet an illusion to infer, as in Rational Psychology, that by means of this Idea we could gain knowledge of the soul as an existent and cognoscible object. In the same way he takes the Idea of the unconditioned without us, and is concerned with a very similar demonstration. After showing that Reason applied to the different forms of conditioned existence in external phenomena must give rise to Ideas of the unconditioned, and thus present to itself the problem of nature of a whole, or the Idea of the Totality of the Universe in space and time, he goes on to show that it is an illusion to take such Idea as giving us knowledge of any existent object corresponding to it. The Idea of the Universe as a whole is an Idea and nothing more, in a word; though a problem Reason necessarily presents to itself for solution, it can never be answered; and when Rational Cosmology takes this Idea and interprets it as an existent object, thereby imagining it has passed beyond experience and gained a conception of the world as a whole, it is nothing more than an illusionary construction—a fact well proved by the contradictions its assertions necessarily give rise to.

But, first, we must understand clearly how the Idea of the Universe or Nature as a whole arises. As we have seen, in the world of experience, every external phenomenon is conditioned by another phenomenon, in accordance with the four classes of categories to which every phenomenon must submit as an object of possible knowledge. In knowledge we are therefore always concerned with a series—(1) a series of adding together, as of parts of space and time; (2) a series of divisions, as of parts of space and time; (3) a series of things arising one from the other, as in causation; and (4) a series of things in dependence one upon the other, under the heading of modality. In every given phenomenon these four series present themselves: for every external phenomenon, as an object of intuition, is an extensive quantity; as an existence that occupies space, it is matter; as a member of the series of the changes of the world, it is an effect; and as one of a series of united links, it is an existence dependent on these links. Otherwise expressed, there is in every phenomenon conditioned quantity, conditioned matter, effect, and dependent existence. Now, as we have seen, wherever conditioned existence is given Reason by its very nature seeks the whole of the conditions, and consequently the absolutely unconditioned, whereby alone the conditioned is possible. Hence, when Reason is applied to the four different series mentioned above—is applied, that is to say, to conditioned quantity, conditioned matter, effect, and dependent existence—it must in each case demand the entire series of conditions, which cannot be complete except they be unconditioned. From a given phenomenon we may thus infer the complete series of its conditions, or the world as a whole. In accordance with the hypothetical syllogism, we may say: given a phenomenon, the series of its conditions (i.e. the world as a whole) is given—is given, that is, as Idea. And in this way the Cosmological Idea, or the Idea of the Universe as a whole, is certainly a right and necessary Idea of Reason ; that is to say, it is a problem which Reason has necessarily to present to itself. But what Kant is mainly concerned with showing is that it is an Idea and nothing more, and that when, as in Rational Cosmology, we take this Idea as having any object corresponding to it, and endeavour thereby to determine the nature of the universe, deciding such questions as whether or not it has a beginning in time or limits in space, we necessarily fall into conflicting assertions, which at once illustrate the nullity of the pretended science.

We now see roughly what the four Cosmological Ideas relate to. In reality they are nothing more than those categories whose synthesis constitutes a series elevated to the unconditioned by Reason demanding absolute totality of conditions in the ascending or regressive series ; and the following will make clear their origin :—

(1) As a quantity, every phenomenon is composite, or extended in space and time. Now phenomena as in time constitutes a series, one time only being determined by relation to a preceding time. And the same applies to space, for though space itself is not serial, the synthesis by which we determine phenomena in space is serial. Reason, then, in its demand for the complete series of all the

CRITICISM OF RATIONAL COSMOLOGY 183

conditions of a given quantity, can only be satisfied with the whole of space and all preceding time; and it thus presents to itself *the complete composition of all phenomena in space and time,* or *the Idea of absolute completeness of Quantity.*

(2) All matter, as existing in space, is divisible or consists of parts; for every space is made up of spaces, and every spatial phenomenon has therefore to be looked upon as made up of parts as conditions of its existence as a whole. The complete series of these conditions which Reason demands are therefore all the parts, which can only be attained by a *completed division.*

(3) Under the heading of Relation, all phenomena as objects in time are determined as effects of causes, which in turn are the effects of prior causes. The complete series of conditions which Reason demands for any given effect are therefore all the causes necessary for its production, or the *completeness of its origin.*

(4) Under the heading of Modality, every dependent existence presupposes another on which it depends. Reason in its demand for unconditioned totality of synthesis can therefore be satisfied only with the *completeness of dependent existence.*

The four Cosmological Ideas, corresponding to the four classes of the categories, thus relate to (1) absolute completeness of composition or quantity, (2) absolute completeness of division, (3) absolute completeness of origination, and (4) absolute completeness of dependence of existence. As stated before, these Ideas are not fictions; they are problems which Reason necessarily presents to itself for solution. But it must always be realised that they are nothing more than this. We may argue: given a conditioned existence (phenomenon), the entire series of its conditions is also given—given *as Idea*. But we may not argue: given a conditioned existence (phenomenon), the complete series of its conditions is given *as object*, as cognoscible object. In the latter argument we are converting the Cosmological Idea into Rational Cosmology; we are concluding from the Idea of the unconditioned that we are able to gain a knowledge of the world as a whole; and that this is quite impossible will be demonstrated in the next section, when we shall show the contradictions all the assertions of Rational Cosmology necessarily give rise to.

The Antinomies of Pure Reason

From the above we see, then, that these Cosmological Ideas are necessary as Ideas or as problems Reason by its very nature presents to itself to be solved. If, however, we let them pass into objects of knowledge, or in other words attempt by the Idea of the Unconditioned to judge of the world as a whole, answering such questions as whether the world has a beginning or has existed from eternity, etc., we are letting the Cosmological Idea become Rational Cosmology, and we then find

CRITICISM OF RATIONAL COSMOLOGY

ourselves enveloped in sophistical propositions, which at once illustrated the nullity of the pretended science. Such propositions are antinomies—assertions which can neither be confirmed nor refuted by experience, but each of which can be proved from pure reason itself. We have thus the extraordinary fact of a "division of pure reason against itself". In all the doctrines of Rational Cosmology it is possible to prove from pure reason that their affirmation is as true as their negation: they are antinomies of pure reason.

Now this, when definitely proved, will demonstrate the impossibility of Rational Cosmology. Indeed, just as we refuted Rational Psychology by exposing the paralogisms on which it was based, so we are now concerned with refuting Rational Cosmology by showing it to be based on antinomies. These antinomies have crossed philosophers throughout the ages, and in his criticism of Rational Cosmology Kant has three things to do in order to clear up the problem. First, he has to establish definitely that they are antinomies, by showing that, whichever of the two alternatives we choose, we are forced into contradictions; secondly, he has to account for them, by showing that they necessarily arise from the nature and relation of our faculties; and thirdly, having shown that the Ideas are unable to extend our knowledge beyond experience, he has to demonstrate what is their purpose with relation to experience.

With regard to the first point, it is not difficult

to see how these antinomies arise. For Reason, when applied to each of the four different forms of the conditioned, demands the complete series of conditions or the " unconditioned totality of phenomenal synthesis ", and this can be reached in two ways—on the one hand, by taking the complete series of conditions as *limited,* òr, on the other, by taking them as *unlimited.* As Caird expresses it, " unconditioned totality of phenomenal synthesis must consist either in a finite or infinite series, in a series which has, or one which has not, a beginning. In the former case, we shall reach totality by discovering the unconditioned condition, which forms the first member of the series ; in the latter case, we shall reach totality by summing up the series of conditions, which, as infinite, is unconditioned." Thus, taking the four Cosmological Ideas already set out, in our attempt to reach totality of phenomenal synthesis we are in each case led into conflicting assertions, for :—

(1) In the *Idea of absolute completeness of quantity,* totality in the synthesis of phenomena in space and time can only be attained by (a) tracing them back to a first and absolute phenomenon in space and time, or (b) by summing up the infinite series of spaces and times and phenomena in them.

(2) In the *Idea of absolute completeness of division,* totality of synthesis can only be attained by (a) reaching simple and indivisible parts, or (b) summing up the infinite series of parts within parts.

(3) In the *Idea of absolute completeness of origina-*

CRITICISM OF RATIONAL COSMOLOGY 187

tion, totality of causal synthesis can only be attained by (a) reaching an absolute (unconditioned) cause, or (b) summing up the infinite series of causes.

(4) In the *Idea of absolute completeness of dependence of existence*, unconditioned totality of synthesis can only be reached by (a) discovering an absolutely necessary being, i.e. an existence containing the conditions of its possibility in itself, or (b) summing up the infinite series of contingent phenomena.

In short, in all cases we take given phenomena, and in seeking for the complete condition by which alone they can be possible, Reason, in its demand for totality of synthesis, can only be satisfied with either (a) an absolute beginning, or (b) a complete infinite series. Indeed, that these two contradictory methods of reaching the unconditioned must arise could be known without demonstration from what we found to be true of Reason; for, if the problems raised by it are to be answered, they can only be answered by the Understanding, and as knowledge given by the Understanding is necessarily of the conditioned, it can never be adequate to the absolute unity and totality of Reason. There is therefore perpetual warfare between the two faculties: for if we take such conception of the Unconditioned as alone is adequate to Reason, it is found too great for the Understanding; and if we take such a conception of it as can be definitely known by the Understanding, it is too small for Reason. We have accordingly to take the complete series of conditions as limited or unlimited, in accordance with whether we regard them as completely cognoscible, or not as completely cognoscible. Hence, when we turn to the four Cosmological Ideas, and letting them pass into Rational Cosmology, try to judge of the world as a whole, we find ourselves faced with the following mutual oppositions, each of which is equally provable :—

ANTINOMY OF PURE REASON
CONFLICT OF THE TRANSCENDENTAL IDEAS

Thesis	*Antithesis*
The world has a beginning in time and bounds in space.	The world has no beginning in time and no limits in space, but is infinite in both time and space.
Every composite substance in the world consists of simple parts; and there exists nothing which is not either itself simple or composed of simple parts.	No composite thing in the world consists of simple parts; and there does not exist in the world any simple substance.
Causality according to the laws of nature is not the only causality operating to originate the phenomena of the world. A causality of freedom (i.e. a cause independent of prior causes) is also necessary to account fully for these phenomena.	There is no such thing as freedom, but everything in the world happens according to the laws of Nature, i.e. is determined.

CRITICISM OF RATIONAL COSMOLOGY

There exists in or in connection with the world—either within it as part of it, or outside it as the cause of it—an absolutely necessary Being.	An absolutely necessary Being does not exist, either within or without the world, as its cause.

We have not the space to describe each of the proofs in these antinomies. Suffice it to say that, with a single exception, Kant's proof on either side consists in taking the opposite for granted and then proving its impossibility. In other words, the method of proof is indirect or apagogic : that is to say, the necessity of a judgment being identical with the impossibility of its contradictory, Kant uses the latter to prove the former ; and in this way the necessity and impossibility of each proposition are alternately established. Thus, in the thesis of the first antinomy, *the world has a beginning in time,* the proof runs : " Granted, that the world has no beginning in time ; up to every given moment of time, an eternity has elapsed, and therewith passed away an infinite series of successful conditions or states of things in the world. Now the infinity of a series consists in the fact, that it never can be completed by means of a successive synthesis. It follows that an infinite series already elapsed is impossible, and that consequently a beginning of the world is a necessary condition of existence." Likewise, if we turn to the antithesis, by granting the opposite and saying " *the world has a beginning*", we can prove this to be impossible and thereby establish our case. Thus :—" Let us assume that the world has a beginning. Then, as beginning is an existence which is preceded by a time in which the thing is not, it would follow that antecedently there was a time in which the world was not, that is, an empty time In an empty time, however, it is impossible that anything should take its beginning, because of such a time no part possesses any condition of existence or non-existence to distinguish it from another (whether produced by itself or through another cause). Hence, though many a series of things may take its beginning in the world, the world itself can have no beginning, and in reference to time past is infinite "

Again, to take the causal antinomy, it is possible in each case to take the opposite, and then prove its impossibility by showing that it contradicts the law of causality itself. Thus, in proof of the thesis, that *there is causality through freedom*, it may be argued that, if everything happens according to the laws of nature, we can never find a first cause, and there is therefore never a sufficient cause for anything that happens—*which contradicts the law of causality*. Likewise, in proof of the antithesis, that *there is no such thing as freedom, but that everything happens according to the laws of nature*, it is easy to suppose that there is a free causality, and then to prove our case by its impossibility. For it may be argued that, if there existed free causality, it must be conceived, not only as beginning the series of causes and effects, but also as determining itself to begin; that is to say, it must be uncaused—*which, again, contradicts the law of causality.* In a word, the principle of causality by its very nature at once posits an absolute beginning, yet renders an absolute beginning impossible; and the necessity and impossibility of each proposition are therefore inevitable.

In all cases except the thesis of the fourth antinomy (which is proved directly) Kant uses this indirect or apagogic method of proof. It is thus simply a question of leading off first. In Kant's own words: " These sophistical assertions open, as it were, a battle-field, where the side obtains the victory which has been permitted to make the attack, and he is compelled to yield who has been unfortunately obliged to stand on the defensive Hence champions of ability, whether on the right or on the wrong side, are certain to carry away the crown of victory, if only they take care to have the right to make the last attack, and are not obliged to sustain another outset from their opponent. We can easily believe that this arena has been often trampled by the feet of the combatants, that many victories have been obtained on both sides, but that the last victory decisive of the affair between the contending parties, was won by him who fought for the right, only if his adversary was forbidden to continue the torney. As impartial umpires, we must lay aside entirely the consideration whether the combatants are fighting for the right or for the wrong side, for the true or for the false, and allow the combat to be first decided. Perhaps, after they have wearied more than injured each other, they will discover the nothingness of their cause of quarrel, and part good friends."

Nevertheless, though these cosmological ideas have no objective validity, they are yet not arbitrary fictions of thought. They are attempts to solve four natural and unavoidable problems of reason. In them we find reason struggling to rise from the region of experience and to soar to sublime ideas, which, if philosophy could support them, would raise it far above all other departments of human knowledge. " The questions : whether the world has a beginning and a limit to its extension in space ; whether there exists anywhere, or perhaps in my own thinking self, an indivisible and indestructible unity—or whether nothing but what is divisible and transitory exists ; whether I am a free agent, or am bound in the chains of nature and fate ; whether, finally, there is a supreme cause of the world, or all our thought and speculation must end with nature and the order of external things—are questions for the solution of which the mathematician would willingly exchange his whole science." But unfortunately speculative reason, in the midst of her highest anticipations, finds herself hemmed in by a press of opposite and contradictory conclusions, from which she cannot withdraw because she herself has been the means of raising them. It is clear that the arrogant claims of both sides in the argument have to be abandoned ; but a brief consideration of the interests involved will explain the fiery zeal of those on the one side and the cold maintenance of their cause of those on the other, why one party has met with the warmest approbation, whilst the other has been repulsed by prejudice.

In dealing, first, with the thesis of each of the antinomies there are three interests to be considered—a *practical* interest, a *speculative* interest, and the interest of *popularity*. Of these, the *practical* (or moral) interest comes before all with humanity. "That the world has a beginning—that the nature of my thinking self is simple, and therefore indestructible—that I am a free agent, and raised above the compulsion of nature and her laws—and finally, that the entire order of things, which form the world, is dependent on a Supreme Being from whom the whole receives unity and connection—these are so many foundation stones of morality and religion". The antithesis deprives us of all these supports, or at least seems to. For if there does not exist a Supreme Being distinct from the world—if the world is without beginning and consequently without a Creator—if our wills are not free, and the soul is divisible and subject to corruption just like matter—the Ideas and principles of morality lose all validity, and fall with the transcendental Ideas which constituted their theoretical support.

The *speculative* interest lies in this: that in knowledge we naturally aim at unity, and we do this in two ways, not only in seeking the complete connection of phenomena themselves, but also in systematically combining our knowledge into a whole of science. As far as the first is concerned, if we assume the Transcendental Ideas in the thesis, we have a sort of goal in which we can regard all our empirical investigations as ending, for we can understand the derivation of the conditioned by referring it to the unconditioned; whereas if we deny the thesis, we have simply to keep following the series of conditions, fully recognising beforehand that they can neither find end nor basis. And in the same way, in combining all our knowledge into a general system, or systematic whole, we have a natural interest in the thesis, for the propositions of the antithesis are of a character that renders the completion of an edifice of cognition impossible. Thus, in both cases all our hopes are centred on the thesis, and none on the antithesis.

The advantage of *popularity* is also on the side of the thesis. To the common understanding the idea of an unconditioned beginning of all syntheses comes quite natural, accustomed as it is to follow out consequences rather than to seek causes. The ideas that the world has a beginning, that there exists a Supreme Being, and that I am a free agent, are not only pleasing to it, but, moreover, are dogmas that cannot be refuted by any experience. Thus, the aid given to speculation, practical interests of great import, and the pleasure of gaseous eloquence without fear of contradiction, with most men settle the question definitely, and even with those who have enough ability to try and consider both sides, the torture of doubt is apt to become too great for them, and they take the side which with one dogmatic belief makes all things clear, instead of continuing for ever the long process of enquiry which the other side involves, and which it can never solve if it goes on for ever.

These three are the interests we have in the thesis or the dogmatism of Pure Reason, but the side of the antithesis or empiricism has a big advantage for all investigation of nature, in that it excludes any chance of explaining phenomena by other than natural means. Here understanding is always upon its proper ground of investigation—the field of experience or possible experience, the laws of which it can explore. The faculty of cognition, in its demands for higher conditions, can find its proper objects; and if in his thread of physical investigations, the empiricist finds a gap, he does not, like a child or a savage, fill it in by suggesting supernatural intervention or free causality, but perseveres in investigation until the missing link is found. Further, the empiricist, far from thinking matters have been brought to satisfactory conclusion at any stage, is compelled to go on investigating for ever (for the conclusion can never be arrived at). In this way, Empiricism not only prevents us from building castles in the air by checking a reason that boasts of insight and knowledge just where both cease to exist, but also keeps the human mind for ever at work in the endless thread of physical investigation, never allowing it to be broken by any admittance of the intervention of the supernatural. Indeed, such interests in favour of the antithesis of the antinomies are so strong that many scientists might reasonably ignore the thesis as being nothing but a source of danger; but when they go further, and becoming dogmatic, deny anything beyond the phenomenal, they are committing the very error they are condemning, and an error, too, that is all the more serious because it does great damage to practical interests. In a word, whilst it is open to ignore the dogmatical propositions, simply saying that they can never be objects of experience, there is utterly no justification in denying them.

Solution of the Four Antinomies

These are the respective interests we have in the two sides of the antinomies, the considerations that tend to make us partisans; but they can in no way influence the issue at stake. The fact remains that, whenever pure reason tries to form a consistent conception of the world as a whole, it finds itself faced with these four conflicts; and whichever side we should like to take, no sooner do we do so than we are contradicted by the other. At first sight we seem, therefore, to be involved

CRITICISM OF RATIONAL COSMOLOGY 197

in an evitable see-saw, and to be compelled to resort to utter scepticism. But Kant insists that this is one of those departments of knowledge where we must necessarily be able to answer every question we raise ; for the problem is not like those suggested by the observation of certain phenomena of nature, where our knowledge is often insufficient to supply the solution, but one raised by the very nature of mind itself, and " the same conception that makes it possible to ask the question, must enable us to answer it." In other words, Kant's contention is that in Rational Cosmology we are not concerned with a problem of experience, but only with ideas which are the product of pure reason, and therefore the same reason that supplies the problem must be capable of solving it. Transcendental Idealism, he states, gives the only solution, and moreover, it is a twofold solution. As we have seen, we know only phenomena, and phenomena consists of the combination of the unknown things-in-themselves and the forms of mind. The former constitute the real world, the latter are the universal attributes mind supplies in making it as we know it. Once we understand this distinction between phenomena and noumena, the four antinomies can be quickly solved. Taking the first two antinomies—with respect to the world being finite or infinite in space and time, and matter consisting of simple parts, on the one hand, or being infinitely divisible, on the other—we see that the fallacy lies in treating phenomena as things-in-themselves. When we know that space and time are only forms of perception, we see that to apply them to the noumenal world, and ask if it is finite or infinite, is absurd ; for space and time do not apply to it at all. And similarly, when we take the phenomenal world and ask the same question, we find we are again only setting up a fictitious problem ; for the world in space and time is never finitely or infinitely extended, but only infinitely extensible ; that is to say, it is only extended so far as it is perceived by mind. Both theses and antitheses are therefore false ; for they both relate to a world in space and time considered independent of experience, and such a world we do not know to exist.

The second pair of antinomies are solved by the same method, only with this additional distinction : that the terms here connected by the principles in question may be heterogeneous, and therefore we are enabled to look for the unconditioned either *within* or *without* the world of experience, whereas in the mathematical antinomies the terms connected were homogeneous and we could only look for it within the world of experience. If, therefore, we apply the theses to things-in-themselves and the antitheses to phenomena, we see that both may be true ; for, though causality (being a necessary form of consciousness) must apply to all phenomena, which must therefore be determined, there is no reason why it should apply to noumena. In this way, the real world may be free and permit of a necessary being ; whereas in the phenomenal world

CRITICISM OF RATIONAL COSMOLOGY 199

causality according to the laws of nature is all, and a necessary being is impossible.

The reasons for the conflicts in all four cases are clear. In the first two we have taken phenomena and noumena, contradictory ideas, and applied the qualities of the former to the latter, and contradiction has resulted; in the second two we have taken ideas that applied to phenomena, on the one hand, and noumena, on the other, are quite justifiable, and brought about contradiction by applying them to phenomena only. Thus, the first two antinomies are false; the second two may both be true.

To be more explicit in this critical solution even at the risk of being tautologous, let us go through the four antinomies more fully. Taking the first antinomy as to the world being finite or infinite in space and time, we see that on applying this to phenomena we are only setting up a fictitious problem in the light of transcendental idealism; for, since the phenomenal world only exists for mind, it cannot be regarded as either finitely or infinitely extended in space and time, but only infinitely extensible; it is extended, that is to say, only so far as it is given in experience, and the world as a whole never can be given in experience. On the other hand, if we apply the question to things-in-themselves, we find we are only applying space and time, which are nothing more than forms of mind, to that which is independent of mind and cannot be known to exist either in space or time.

Similarly with respect to the second antinomy. On the one hand, if we take phenomena and try to decide whether there is a limit to the parts we can divide it into (atoms) or whether we can go on dividing for ever, we find that (in the light of transcendental idealism) it is an impossible question; for the parts only exist as given in experience, and do not extend further than experience reaches. On the other hand, if we apply the question to things-in-themselves, we are simply applying the forms of mind, space and time, to what is independent of these. In both the mathematical antinomies we have therefore taken phenomena and things-in-themselves, contradictory ideas, and tried to represent them as capable of union in an idea. When the world is critically understood as capable of division into phenomena and noumena, we see that there is no justification for either the thesis or antithesis in these two antinomies, and that the only solution is that both are therefore false because based on false hypotheses.

The two dynamical antinomies are solved in the same critical manner, but here a dilemma may be avoided. For, whereas in the mathematical antinomies we were concerned with homogeneous terms and could therefore only look for the Unconditioned in the sphere and under the conditions of experience (thus being forced into contradiction), in the present instance we are concerned with terms which may be heterogeneous, and it is therefore possible to look for the unconditioned either *within* or *without* the world of experience. Here, if we take the phenomenal world and ask whether one cause can be free of another, we naturally find it cannot; in the causal chain one phenomenon will necessarily depend on another throughout the whole world of experience, because here mind is part of what appears, and we cannot think otherwise than in terms of causality. But, on the other hand, if we apply the same question to the world as it is in itself, we see that we are again only applying causality, a form of mind, to what is independent of mind and may for all we know be perfectly capable of free causes, causes arising quite independent of one another. And the same applies to the antinomy of contingent and necessary being. In this way, though in phenomena contingent being and causality according to the laws of nature are all and freedom and a necessary being are impossible, the noumenal world may permit of free causes and also a necessary being. Theses and antitheses in these two antinomies may therefore *both* be true when conceived as of noumena, on the one hand, and phenomena, on the other. The apparent contradiction has arisen from taking phenomena as real, and thus applying to noumena ideas only true of phenomena.

Such is the Kantian solution of the antinomies, and, as Kant claimed, nothing is more calculated to make most people believe in Transcendental Idealism than this. If we take the world as we know it to be real and try to form a consistent conception of it as a whole, we find ourselves faced with overwhelming and inevitable contradictions; but if we are content to regard it as a phenomenal world, the contradiction vanishes, and reason, recognising its limitation, is at peace with itself.

Kant has now completed the first two of his three tasks in relation to the Cosmological Ideas. First, he has shown that whenever we let the Cosmological Ideas pass into Rational Cosmology, and endeavour by means of the Idea of the Unconditioned to judge of the world as a whole, we necessarily fall into antinomies, all of which he has proved as such. Secondly, he has found the solution of these antinomies, in that he has accounted for them by showing that they arise from the nature and relation of our faculties. Having thus decided that the Ideas are unable to extend our knowledge beyond experience, his only remaining task is to explain what is their use in relation to experience, and this will be fairly clear from what has already been said. Indeed, though the Ideas have been shown to be in no sense *constitutive* principles, either in relation to experience or beyond experience, no one can fail to see that they have a useful and necessary function as *regulative* principles, in that under their guidance and by dint of them we are compelled to keep seeking higher or more general conditions in the world of experience. For the principle of Reason by which the Ideas were presented as problems to be solved was this: given

CRITICISM OF RATIONAL COSMOLOGY 203

the conditioned, Reason by its very nature seeks the entire series of conditions, whereby alone the conditioned is possible; and it is precisely this demand for the entire series of regressive conditions for every form of conditioned experience that keeps us for ever pursuing our empirical investigations, thus enlarging and extending our knowledge. In Kant's words, " the principle of reason is properly a mere rule—prescribing a regress in the series of conditions for given phenomena, and prohibiting any pause or rest on an absolutely unconditioned. It is, therefore, not a principle of the possibility of experience or of the empirical cognition of sensuous objects.—Still less is it a *constitutive principle* of reason authorising us to extend our conception of the sensuous world beyond all possible experience. It is merely a principle for the enlargement and extention of experience as far as is possible for human faculties. It forbids us to consider any empirical limits as possible. It is, hence, a principle of reason, which, as a rule, dictates how we ought to proceed in our empirical regress, but is unable to anticipate or indicate prior to the empirical regress what is given in the object itself." In a word, the principle of Reason is not *constitutive* but *regulative*. It does not enable us to anticipate what will be discovered in experience, and least of all to gain knowledge of objects transcending experience; it merely directs us to widen and extend our experience to the utmost, and with this its purpose begins and ends.

Compatibility of Freedom and Necessity

It is perhaps advisable to deal with the solution of the Causal Antinomy more fully, for it supplies what is probably the strongest defence of the possibility of free-will that philosophy can produce. The thesis of this antinomy, it will be remembered, was: *Causality according to the laws of nature is not the only causality operating to originate the phenomena of the world. A causality of freedom is also necessary to account fully for these phenomena.* On the other hand, the antithesis was to the effect that: *There is no such thing as freedom, but everything in the world happens according to the laws of nature.*

Dealing first with the antithesis, in the phenomenal world no one can deny the law of causality. In the world as we know it every phenomenon is conditioned by some other phenomenon; every effect has its cause, that cause is again only the effect of some prior cause, and however far we pass down the causal chain we shall never find the primal cause. And we cannot think otherwise. Phenomenally, then, the universe appears mechanistic, a clock put together and wound up. Hence moral freedom is impossible; man's volitions are simply links in the causal chain. But we naturally ask: Can such a state be true of the world? Does not common sense and subjective knowledge deny it? Scientifically determinism would certainly appear true of the universe, psychologically it would appear true of human nature; for from causality there is no escape, not even in dreams. But common sense denies it, and so we turn to the thesis of the antinomy, and ask, What do we really mean when we speak of freedom? We find that we mean a faculty of spontaneously originating a state, the cause of which is not subordinated to another cause determining it in time; that is to say, a state that can begin to act of itself, without any cause determining it to action according to the law of causality. In the practical sense it is the independence of the will of coercion by sensuous impulses—a faculty of self determination. Such a conception is a transcendental idea, but we never start to doubt it until we learn that things in the world as we know it are determined by the law of causality. We then see that we are involved in a contradiction, and since we cannot sacrifice the law of causality and want also to retain freedom, we at once ask if there is not some way in which freedom can be compatible with natural necessity, or whether the law of causality must of necessity exclude it. In other words, do we enounce a contradictory proposition when we say that every effect must have its origin either in nature or in freedom? Or is it not possible that both can exist together in the same event in different relations? The principle of an unbroken connection between all events in the phenomenal world, in accordance with the unchangeable laws of nature, is a well established principle which admits of no exception.

The question, therefore, is: "Whether an effect, determined according to the laws of nature, can at the same time be produced by a free agent, or whether freedom and nature mutually exclude each other."

Now if we conceive-phenomena as being absolute reality, if the world as known exists as such independent of mind, then the compatibility of freedom and necessity is impossible, says Kant. "In this case nature is the complete and all-sufficient cause of every event, and condition and conditioned, cause and effect, are contained in the same series and necessitated by the same law"; and so the world is determined. If, on the contrary, phenomena are held, as in this philosophy, to be nothing more than mere representations, connected with each other in accordance with empirical laws, there must be noumena " behind " them, and the law of causality not applying to noumena but being only a condition of consciousness, there is no reason why such noumena should not be free. In so far as noumena are the unknowable ground of phenomena Kant calls them the *intelligible* or non-sensuous cause, in that it is outside space and time; it exists out of and apart from the series of phenomena, but its effects are to be found in the series of phenomena. Such effects in relation to their intelligible cause may therefore be considered free, though in relation to phenomena they must follow as the direct and determined effect of preceding phenomena. In this way, if a sensuous object

CRITICISM OF RATIONAL COSMOLOGY 207

possesses an intelligible or non-sensuous faculty by which it can give birth to phenomena, the causality of such an object may be regarded from two different points of view. As regards the *cause* of its action which is noumenal, it may be considered to be intelligible; as regards its *effects*, which become part of the phenomenal world, it can be regarded as sensuous. Accordingly we have to form both an intellectual and empirical conception of the causality of such a faculty, both however having reference to the same effect. The one may be regarded as the object's character as thing-in-itself, the latter its character as a phenomenon. Now in its character as thing-in-itself, such an object would not be subordinate to the conditions of time, time being only a condition of phenomena. No action would *begin* or *cease to be* in this object; so it would be free from the law of change, by which everything which happens must have a cause in the preceding phenomena. Thus, it would *determine and not be determined*. Again, this intelligible character would not be cognised, because we can perceive nothing but phenomena; yet, on the other hand, its character as phenomena would fall in line with the law of causality and would appear to follow as the result of the preceding phenomena, thus being phenomenally determined. In this way nature and freedom, understood critically, could exist without contradiction in the same event.

The Freedom of the Will

We now come to apply the solution of the Causal antinomy to man's conduct—to decide the question of freedom and determinism on the ground set out above. Phenomenally all the acts of a man must take their place in the causal chain and therefore appear determined. In the sense world a free cause is impossible; hence the idea of freedom of the will cannot have come from external experience. It is a transcendental idea, but for all that the idea is in the meanest intelligence. The man in the street regards himself as a free agent, holding himself responsible for his actions and agreeing that he is deserving of blame when he does wrong. It is the business of philosophy to show how this freedom may be possible, even though science and empirical psychology show it to be impossible. It must demonstrate that a freedom of choice of action on man's part is, at any rate, compatible with the well established and universal law of phenomenal necessity.

The question we have to ask ourselves is this: Although every effect in the phenomenal world must be connected with an empirical cause (the universal law of nature), may it not be that in man's case this empirical causality is itself the effect of a non-empirical and intelligible causality—its connection with the natural causes remaining nevertheless intact? Now Kant's contention is that man is an *intelligible* being, in that, though a

CRITICISM OF RATIONAL COSMOLOGY 209

sensuous object, he possesses an intelligible or nonsensuous faculty by which he can give birth to phenomena; namely, his understanding and reason, in respect of which he is self-determining and not fatally influenced by sensuous conditions. It is true that in human action one phenomenon must certainly appear the cause of the other phenomenon, considered empirically; yet the true cause of such causal phenomenon is transcendentally reason, pure thought, which is self originated and not caused by other phenomena, though it must always appear to be. Thus man is, on the one hand, a phenomenon of the sensuous world, and therefore a link in the causal chain; but, on the other, he is an intelligible being, himself causing the phenomenon which forms the link in such chain. Man cognises himself not only by his senses (as phenomenon), but also through pure apperception, in actions and internal determinations; and in respect of this latter he knows himself as an intelligible object—intelligible because his actions cannot be ascribed to sensuous receptivity. Thus, man's reason may be able to originate an action independent of any causal phenomena (for reason is thing-in-itself and unaffected by forms of the sense world); yet the action itself will be a phenomenon, and appear to fall in line with an unbroken causal chain. In other words, though the empirical character in human action appears to have been caused by some other empirical character, it is really determined by an intelligible character, and this intelligible character we cannot perceive ; we can only know its empirical character. It cannot be said of reason, then, that the state in which it determines the will is always preceded by some other state determining it ; for reason is not subject to sensuous conditions. The causality of reason in its intelligible character does not begin to be ; it does not make its appearance at a certain time, for the purpose of producing an effect. Reason must be regarded as a positive faculty which can spontaneously originate a series of events, *determining and not determinable*.

That reason possesses this faculty of causality, this power of starting a causal series independent of other causes, is evident from the fact that the average man is always conscious of the *I ought* in all practical affairs. Since phenomenally considered the world is determined, this moral imperative, *I ought*, cannot have come from external experience of nature, for the external world would simply contradict my chances of being able to do otherwise than go in a determined course. The idea of an *ought*, or of duty, arises from a pure internal conception ; for whatever number of motives nature may present to my will, whatever sensuous impulses, the moral *ought* is beyond their power to produce.

Expressed in a few words, Kant's position is this. Man's voluntary actions are the effect of pure reason, of his intelligible character ; hence he may be a free agent, not a mere link in the causal chain. Yet Man's acts themselves, looked at as phenomena, are absolutely determined. In other words, man may be a free agent because he can originate acts ; but when we view these acts the very nature of our minds compels us to weave them into the phenomenal causal chain, making them the determined effects of various phenomenal causes. But such " causes " are not the real cause ; the real cause is reason, which, being non-sensuous, is free and not the puppet of the phenomenal causes.

In this way, whilst not pretending to prove freedom, Kant defends the possibility of freedom, which he considered was the most the intellect could ever accomplish.

CHAPTER III

THE IDEA OF GOD.

Kant's Refutation of Rational Theology

WE have now completed the first two divisions of the Dialectic, the Psychological and Cosmological Ideas; the third constitutes what Kant calls the Ideal of Pure Reason, or the Idea of God. Kant's treatment of this Idea divides itself into two parts: first, the origin and nature of the Idea, and, secondly, a criticism of the proofs by which it is endeavoured to prove its objective validity, or to establish the existence of a Being corresponding to the Idea. In first part he is concerned with establishing that the nature of consciousness is such that Reason necessarily presents to itself the conception of God, which is therefore not a fiction but a necessary Idea of Reason. But we have to remember that it is an Idea and nothing more; and in the second part he proceeds to demonstrate that when, as in Rational Theology, we take the Idea as having an object corresponding to it, and by rational proofs seek to establish the existence of God, we find that all such proofs necessarily fail us. In a word, the Idea of God, like the Ideas of the Soul

THE IDEA OF GOD

and the Universe, is perfectly valid as Idea, or as a problem Reason necessarily presents to itself for solution; but if we take the Idea as giving us knowledge of any existent object corresponding to it, we are allowing Reason to become dialectical; and just as Kant refuted Rational Psychology by showing it to be based on paralogisms and Rational Cosmology by proving its assertions to be antinomies, so he now refutes Rational Theology by establishing the necessary impossibility of all its proofs.

But, first, how does the Idea of God arise? To understand Kant's treatment of the nature and origin of this Idea we must realise that here, as in all other parts of the Critique, he is concerned with showing a transcendental synthetical parallel to the analytical laws of logic. Indeed, just as he had previously shown the unity of apperception to afford a synthetical principle parallel to $A=A$, so he now takes the law of Excluded Middle (as the principle of disjunctive syllogisms), and is concerned with showing that the Idea of God is the product of a transcendental parallel to this. Now the logical law of Excluded Middle enables us to say that every concept can be determined by one of two contradictory predicates, one of which it must contain. We can always lay down with certainty that " A is or is not B ", whatever A or B may symbolize; and if all possible predicates are given us, a concept may be determined by all its attributes thoroughly. But this purely logical principle has nothing to do with the *content* of a conception, or the reality or unreality of the thing which is the subject of predication. The proposition " A is or is not B " is merely concerned with logical affirmation or negation ; it tells us nothing at all about the existence or non-existence of A, but only what is contained in the conception of it. Kant therefore holds that beyond this formal principle, showing how things are possible as objects of thought, there must be a transcendental principle of the complete determination of them as objects of knowledge. In other words, if the content of a concept is to be determined, as well as the logical form of cognition, the opposed predicates must not merely affirm or deny attributes ; they must be determinate of being and non-being—their affirmation referring to positive existence, their negation to its absence, want, or limit. In this light, then, we are entitled to say that everything must be determined positively or negatively in relation to every possible predicate ; and this assertion " involves more than the principle of contradiction, for it contemplates not merely the relation of two contradictory predicates of a thing, but also the relation of the thing to the whole compass of possibility, as the sum-total of all the predicates of things." It means that I cannot think of anything as existing without putting it in relation to a whole of possible experience ; that in order to know anything completely, I must know all that is possible, and determine the object in relation to that knowledge either positively or negatively. At the basis of every object of experience there is thus presupposed a transcendental substratum—a substratum which is to form the fund from which all possible predicates of things are to be supplied, namely, the idea of a sum-total of reality to the exclusion of all negation. To set an object before our minds is to determine it by predicates in relation to this idea of all reality— the number of positive predicates by which the object is determined denoting the amount of existence it contains, its negative predicates the absence or want of the same. Accordingly, since it is by limiting this a priori idea that we determine the objects of experience, we naturally look upon it as a thing in itself constituting the material of all possibility, or the ground of the possibility of all finite things. Further, since the exclusion of all negation, which the idea of all reality demands, means the exclusion of all opposition and reciprocal limitation, this material of all possibility has to be regarded as simple or as an individual being. And in this way, we " find ourselves authorised to determine our notion of the Supreme Being by means of the mere conception of the highest reality, as one simple, all-sufficient, eternal and so on—in one word, to determine it in unconditioned completeness by the aid of every possible predicate. The conception of such a being is the conception of God in its transcendental sense, and thus the ideal of reason is the object of a transcendental Theology."

In this way, then, the concept of Deity is determined. We have necessarily to conceive it as the sum-total of all possible predicates, and, as negative predicates only imply the absence or want of positive ones, this means the sum-total of all possible predicates or of all realities. Only the individual or singular object can contain all attributes—species and genera only contain a part of the individual, and the higher and more universal concepts become the less they contain. Hence, as the concept of God is only to be thought as the sum of all realities, it is necessarily represented as individual, or as a single Being. Kant calls this Idea the Ideal of Pure Reason—the only one pure reason is capable of. It is not imagination that invents the idea, but pure reason which necessarily produces it in forming its conception of Deity, and as long as the Ideal aims at being nothing more than an Idea, or a problem Reason necessarily presents to itself for solution, it is perfectly valid. When, however, the Idea is allowed to pass into an object, or is regarded as having an existent Being corresponding to it, Reason has become dogmatic. In this case the theological Idea has passed into Rational Theology; it has become the object of a science whose endeavour is to prove the real existence of God. The Critique is concerned with the investigation of the proofs put forward by this alleged science. If they are shown to be impossible, Rational Theology will have shared the same fate as Rational Psychology and Rational Cosmology. It will have been shown to be impossible as a science, and the Theological Idea, though necessary as Idea or problem Reason presents to itself for solution, will have been found incapable of solution.

THE GENERAL PROBLEM OF RATIONAL THEOLOGY

Now all Rational Theology, or logical demonstration of the existence of God, lies in establishing the combination of two conceptions—the conception of an ens realissimum and the conception of necessary being. Here two courses are open: either to take the concept of the most real being and prove that it necessarily exists, or to prove of necessary existence that it constitutes the most real being. In the first case our proof is entirely a priori, or ontological: we seek to show that the rational Idea of God is such that its very nature necessarily implies objective existence. In the second case our proof is empirical (in its start, at any rate): for starting with the conditioned existence of experience, we seek to establish necessary existence, and thence to prove that this necessary existence constitutes the most real being. Whichever course we adopt the end desired is the same; both arguments converge, or seek to converge, in the demonstration of the existence of the ens realissimum.

The course humanity most naturally takes in its demonstration of the existence of God is the latter. Starting with experience, we find that every object is contingent; it only exists under the condition of some other thing, which is its cause, and from this we go on to conclude the existence of a cause which is not contingent, but exists necessarily and unconditionally. Accordingly, Reason searches for the conception adequate to such necessary being; that is to say, it looks for the conception of a being such as possesses no element inconsistent with the idea of absolute necessity. It can only find it in that which contains a *therefore* to every *wherefore*, or is itself the sufficient condition of all other things —a being, that is to say, which constitutes the unconditioned source of every positive attribute found in the world : *every* attribute because if any attribute in the world were not contained in it, that attribute would necessarily remain unexplained, and *positive* as opposed to negative attributes because negative attributes cannot form part of reality, but are only to be regarded as mere defects or absence of reality. Reason thus becomes convinced that the only conception consistent with its demand for absolute necessity is a being forming the sum of all positive reality to the exclusion of all negation, or in philosophical language an ens realissimum. As previously explained, such a being must be individual, all-sufficient, eternal, etc.—in a word, determined in unconditioned perfection under every possible category; and it is on such reasoning that we regard the existence of God as an all-powerful and all-perfect Being as having been established.

Now Kant admits that, if it were absolutely necessary to make up our mind one way or another

THE IDEA OF GOD

as to the nature of necessary Being, we should have to decide that it is the ens realissimum ; for only a Being that contains all reality in itself can be seen from the very idea of it to be necessary. But apart from practical considerations (with which we are not now concerned) we are not so obliged to make up our minds, and, considered strictly, the argument has logical defects. For even admitting the step from contingent to necessary being (which is particularly contrary to the critical philosophy), we cannot say that the ens realissimum is the only being that is absolutely necessary. There is no contradiction in supposing a limited being to be necessary, and the fact that it is possible that necessity might be conjoined with finitude renders the identification of the necessary being with the ens realissimum an argument that is not watertight. Our attempt to prove of necessary existence that it constitutes the most real being therefore fails. Though the argument starts from experience, it is really one of pure conceptions. Experience only aids us in making one step—to the existence of a necessary being. What the properties of such a being are, we cannot learn from experience ; therefore reason abandons it altogether, and pursues its enquiries in the sphere of pure conceptions, for the purpose of discovering what the properties of an absolutely necessary being ought to be. Reason believes that it has discovered these requisites in the conception of an ens realissimum, and hence concludes that the ens realissimum is an absolutely necessary being. But it is evident that reason has here presupposed that the conception of an ens realissimum is perfectly adequate to the conception of a being of absolute necessity; that is, that we may infer the existence of the latter from that of the former—which is simply the a priori or ontological argument. In other words, to prove of necessary existence that it constitutes the most real being is ultimately to prove of the conception of the most real being that it necessarily exists. In each case our argument is equally ontological; and it thus becomes clear that the burden of proving the existence of God must depend entirely on the a priori argument, and that experience can really play no part in the matter. All this will be made clearer in the next section, however. We shall there deal separately with Kant's treatment of each of the logical arguments by which Rational Theology has endeavoured to establish its case, and shall show how ultimately they all have to fall back on to the Ontological argument, which in turn is inadequate to the burden.

Refutation of all Rational Theology

Throughout the history of thought many attempts have been made to logically prove the existence of God but in reality all such rational " proofs " resolve themselves into three :—(1) The Teleological or Physico-theological argument, from the evidence of design in nature to an intelligent, purposive First Cause or Creator ; (2) the Cosmological argument, from the contingent existence of things actual to the existence of a necessary being containing all reality as their ground; (3) the Ontological or a priori argument, from the very nature of the concept or idea of Deity. These are the only possible arguments of the purely intellectual type, but as Kant points out, when they are thoroughly examined, the first is found to need the support of the second, and the second the support of the third; so that ultimately all depends on the validity of this third argument. Thus, the teleological argument, though apparently very striking and forcible, at the most cannot prove more than a world architect, Kant explains; if we want to prove that this architect is the creator of the material he works with, we have to fall back on the argument from contingent to necessary existence; and, if this necessary existence is to be proved the Being inclusive of all reality and perfection, the support of the ontological argument is required. The whole question thus depends on the ontological argument; if this fails, rational proof of the existence of God becomes impossible.

This will become clearer if we deal with the various arguments more specifically. Taking first the Teleological (or Physico-theological) argument, Kant admits that this "will always deserve to be mentioned with respect", because "it is the oldest, the clearest and simplest of all, and imparts life to the study of nature." It is the argument from design. Man finds a watch or a ship, and he knows them to be the work of a watchmaker or shipbuilder, who has pieced together their various pieces regarding each as a means to a definite end. He finds also a world opening to his view a magnificent spectacle of order, variety, beauty and conformity to ends; indeed, whether he pursues his observations into the infinity of space, on the one side, or its illimitable divisions, on the other, he encounters such a chain of causes and effects, of means and ends, birth and death, and all so harmoniously united and wonderfully beautiful, that his astonishment is beyond expression and dumbness his only eloquence. The whole world manifests signs of an arrangement full of purpose; and since this purposeful order is not necessary to the existence of the things of the world taken each by itself, but is rather a foreign attribute accidentally attached to them, it is argued that the co-operation of things to the attainment of definite ends could not have come about if they had not been selected and arranged in relation to those ends by a rational principle acting under the guidance of ideas. Man, therefore, concludes that there exists a sublime and wise cause or causes, which cannot be found in the mere productive energy of an all powerful but blindly working nature, but must be found in the freedom of an intelligent agent—an agent whose unity of purpose may be inferred from the unity of the parts of the world in their reciprocal relations as members of the complete and purposive whole. What is to prevent him from conceiving such agent to be a Supreme Author, in whom all possible perfection is embodied as in a single substance?

We have here an argument from analogy. Just as man's watch or ship was the work of a designing intelligence, who pieced together his product bit by bit with an ultimate purpose, so, it is concluded, the connection or harmony of the Universe can only find its explanation in a similar cause, and an attempt is made to proportion the greatness of the cause according to the effect. True, it may be pointed out that the purposiveness of nature is an artistic assumption rather than a scientifically proved fact, and that, even conceding such harmony and order, much of it can be explained on mechanistic principles; but in relation to the whole such considerations appear minor, and man cannot on this account sacrifice his teleological idea of the world, by which alone he can interpret nature as a whole and in accordance with his religious consciousness. Nor does Kant, indeed, think it would be reasonable for him to do so. He is willing to concede all the harmonious unity, and regard it, if you like, as the work of a designing intelligence; but granting all this, the argument only proves an *architect*, never a *creator* of the world, he states. It explains the form and order in the world, but the origin of its matter or substance can never be accounted for on such lines. In all cases of human construction the material worked with is always given to the designer, not made by him, and similarly in the case of Nature, the unspeakable designing power of the architect does not prove the matter of the world to be created by the architect or that such architect is one and absolute. We may infer, it is true, a cause equal to the effect, and we may also conclude that only a single power combined with great wisdom could have produced the effects found in the world. But how can we decide the extent of the power and wisdom? Who can measure the proportion between cause and effect, and decide how great the perfection of the world-arranging cause must be in order to be adequate to the existing effects? To say that the perfection must be very great, far above all human perfection, would be an idle assertion, leaving the matter quite undetermined. For it would be merely to determine God by relation to the mind of the observer of nature and the standard of that mind, and such a relative greatness may be attributed to the lowness of that standard quite as much as to the loftiness of the object compared with it. God can be nothing definite unless He be all-powerful and all-perfect—in a word, defined under the category of totality. But such totality can never be reached by an empirical process; we cannot say what is "the relation of the greatness of the world, as we have observed it, to perfect wisdom, or what is the relation of the unity of the world, as we have observed it, to absolute unity." If we are to proceed from empirical multiplicity to totality, we must give up the notion of a proportionate cause to the effects found in the world;

there is only one way open to us, and that is to show that the contingent implies the necessary being, and that this necessary being, as such, must be the ens realissimum. But this simply means that the argument has ceased to be the teleological argument, based on design in nature, and has become the cosmological argument, inferring from the contingent being of existence, necessary being inclusive of all reality as its ground. In other words, whatever disadvantages the cosmological argument may be found to have, the teleological argument has all these disadvantages, together with the quite additional ones of its own.

THE COSMOLOGICAL ARGUMENT

Now the cosmological argument starts from the contingency of all objects of experience. In effect it says: contingent things exist—at least, I myself exist—and as such things are not self caused and cannot be explained by an infinite series, it follows that there must be a necessary being, by which alone the contingent is possible. Now only one type of being can be seen from its very nature to be necessary, namely, a being containing all reality in itself; hence (concludes the argument) the necessary being must be of this nature, or, in other words, an ens realissimum or God. The argument thus divides itself into two steps: first, the step from contingent to necessary being, and, secondly, the establishing of this necessary being to be the ens realissimum. The first step is based on the law of causality. Everything which is contingent has a cause; this cause has likewise a cause, and so on and so on, until finally the series of subordinate causes must end with an absolutely necessary cause, without which it would not possess completeness. Having got this far, and convinced itself that necessary or unconditional being must exist, Reason next asks itself : What kind of being is there that from its very nature is seen to be necessary, or, in other words, contains no element inconsistent with the idea of absolute necessity? It can only find it in that which in itself is the unconditioned source of every positive attribute found in the world, or a being which contains all reality in itself; and thus it concludes that the necessary being must be the ens realissimum or God.

Now though this mode of arguing is a perfectly natural one to the human mind, we need not examine it very closely to see that it involves many dogmatic assumptions—both in its step from contingent to necessary being, and its conclusion that this necessary being must be God or a being containing all reality in itself. Dealing with the first step, it is clear that, in the first place, it confuses phenomena with things in themselves, in that it uses the category of causality, which only applies to the former, to give an explanation of the latter—a step quite contrary to the critical philosophy. And in the second place, it takes the idea of absolute necessity, an Idea of Pure Reason only, as itself an established object of knowledge, and from the supposed impossibility of an infinite series, it concludes the existence of necessary being. But in so doing it is only taking sides in the antinomy of contingent and necessary being, explained in the last chapter. The statement that there exists a necessary being was the thesis of this antinomy, it will be remembered; the statement that the series was infinite was the antithesis: hence, neither side could be taken without finding itself contradicted by the other. Transcendental Idealism, it is true, offered a solution, in that it showed that though a necessary being was impossible in the world of phenomena, it *may* be possible of noumena. But possibility is not proof, and by no possible means can the existence of a necessary being be established.

So much for the dialectical assumptions in the first step in our argument—the step from contingent to necessary being. But even if we waive these, and assume that the necessary being exists, Kant still holds that our argument is inadequate in that it fails to prove that this necessary being must be the ens realissimum. It is true that only a Being that contains all reality in itself can be seen from the very idea of it to be necessary, but we cannot say that the ens realissimum is the only being that is absolutely necessary. There is no contradiction in supposing a limited being to be necessary, and the possibility that necessity may be conjoined with finitude precludes us from necessarily thinking that the necessary being must be identified with the ens realissimum. Besides, how do we infer of necessary existence that it constitutes the most real being? Simply from the concept. But, as briefly explained before, if from the concept we can prove of necessary existence that it constitutes the most real being, then the proposition must be convertible and we must be able to prove of the most real being that it necessarily exists. In other words, the second part of the cosmological argument is really ontological: it is not a matter of experience at all, but entirely of conception. "Experience," says Kant, "merely aids reason in making one step—to the existence of necessary being. What the properties of this being are, cannot be learned from experience; and therefore reason abandons it altogether, and pursues its enquiries in the sphere of pure conceptions, for the purpose of discovering what the properties of an absolutely necessary being ought to be, that is, what among all possible things contain the conditions of absolute necessity." (i.e. What is there without which a being would not be absolutely necessary?) "Reason believes that it has discovered these requisites in the conception of an ens realissimum, and in it alone, and hence concludes: The ens realissimum is an absolutely necessary being. But it is evident that reason has here presupposed that the conception of an ens realissimum is perfectly adequate to the conception of a being of absolute necessity, that is, that we may infer the existence of the latter from that of the former—*a proposition which formed the basis of the ontological argument,* and which is now employed in the support of the cosmological argument, contrary to the wish and professions of its inventors. For the existence of an absolutely necessary being is given in conceptions alone. But if I say—the conception of the ens realissimum is a conception of this kind, and in fact the only conception which is adequate to our idea of a necessary being, I am obliged to admit that the latter may be inferred from the former. Thus, it is properly the ontological argument which figures in the cosmological and constitutes the whole strength of the latter; while the spurious basis of experience has been of no further use than to conduct us to the conception of absolute necessity, being utterly insufficient to demonstrate the presence of this attribute in any determinate existence or thing."

The Ontological Argument

In this way, it becomes evident that the entire burden of logically proving the existence of a Supreme Being depends on the validity of the Ontological argument—on whether the Ens Realissimum must necessarily be because we conceive it. This argument was first formulated by Anselm, of Canterbury, and later used by Descartes and Leibniz. In effect, the proof as presented by Anselm is as follows:—

(1) God is by definition the most perfect being.
(2) Now existence is an attribute of perfection.

(3) Therefore, anything which had all the other attributes we commonly ascribe to God and yet lacked existence would be less perfect than something which had those attributes, plus that of existence.

(4) So anything which had all the other attributes of God, but did not exist, could not be the most perfect being.

(5) Therefore, the most perfect being (ens realissimum) must exist, besides having the other attributes specified.

(6) But, by definition, God is the most perfect being.

(7) Therefore, by definition, God exists.

It will thus be seen that the argument comes back to this: that the very conception of God as a supremely perfect being implies existence, because (once we have defined God thus) to say that He did not exist would be a contradiction, existence being a necessary attribute of perfection. In other words, having defined God as an all-perfect being, we cannot say He does not exist; because a supremely perfect being who did not exist would be lacking in a quality of perfection (i.e. existence), and our conception would be a contradiction in terms. As is well known, Descartes accepted this proof without more ado, but Leibniz held that, before doing so, it was necessary to make a certain addition, in that it was essential to show that the idea of God was not a contradictory idea, i.e., that it did not contain contradictory attributes. He pointed out that we often find in our minds ideas whose elements, though at first sight harmonious, are found on critical examination to be incompatible. We speak, for instance, of the "greatest possible number" or the "swiftest possible motion", but in reality the "greatest possible" is not compatible with the idea of number, and the "swiftest possible" is not compatible with the idea of motion; for it is always possible to conceive a greater than any particular number and a velocity greater than any specified one. And so it may be with the idea of God. Hence Leibniz held that we must first examine what attributes are essential to the nature of God to see if they are not contradictory; if they are not, it will certainly show that God is possible, and if he is possible, he must exist.

Now Leibniz argues in this fashion: the conception of God as the primal being and source of all being and perfection contains every possible quality without limitation, for limitation is always a type of imperfection (being an absence of a certain positive predicate); hence the conception of God cannot permit of any negative predicates. In other words, not A, whatever positive predicate A may be taken to mean, cannot possibly be thought of a God containing all reality; and, accordingly, the conception of God, being entirely without negative predicates, cannot possibly be a contradictory conception. God as the Being in whom infinite reality is included is therefore possible, and since existence is included in the notion of all reality, God must exist.

Can this argument be regarded as valid, or must we reject it like the others? Kant has no doubt on the matter. Indeed, he states that but for the fact that the second part of the Cosmological argument—the conception that necessary being must be a being containing all reality in itself—is a convertible proposition, the Ontological argument, with its attempt to extract being out of thought, could never have been invented. Philosophers, however, have been deluded by logical necessity, which they have confused with being, says Kant. Every geometrical proposition—a triangle has three angles—is absolutely necessary; and in the same way, it has been held that God as the being inclusive of all reality must necessarily be existent. But the unconditioned necessity of a judgment does not form the absolute necessity of a thing. To suppose the existence of God as the being inclusive of all reality and then to deny that He necessarily exists would be a contradiction, just as it would be a contradiction to suppose a triangle and to deny that it has three angles; for in all judgment, if one annihilates the predicate in thought and retains the subject, a contradiction results. But if one suppresses both subject and predicate in thought, no contradiction is possible, for there is then nothing to form a contradiction out of. In other words, to suppose a triangle and deny it having three angles would certainly be contradictory; but to suppose the non-existence of both triangle and angles is perfectly admissible. And

THE IDEA OF GOD

so with the conception of a necessary Being. Annihilate its existence in thought, and you annihilate the thing itself with all its predicates; and there is then no room for contradiction.

In reply to this, the opposition urge that there are some subjects which we cannot think away, and whose existence is presupposed in the thought of them. And they assert that this in the case of God, who is held to be the one subject it is a contradiction to suppose non-existent. But Kant replies it is absurd to introduce into the conception of a thing, which is to be cogitated solely in reference to its possibility, the conception of its existence. It is simply to confuse the copula, expressing the position of a predicate in relation to a subject, with the verb of existence, expressing the absolute position of the subject itself. The real issue at stake is simply this: Is the assertion *this or that thing exists*, an analytical or a synthetical proposition? "If the former, there is no addition made to the subject of your thought by the affirmation of its existence; but then the conception in your mind is identical with the thing itself, or you have supposed the existence of a thing to be possible, and then referred its existence from its internal possibility—which is but a miserable tautology. The word *reality* in the conception of the thing, and the word *existence* in the conception of the predicate, will not help you out of the difficulty. For, supposing you were to term all positing of a thing *reality*, you have thereby posited the thing with all its predicates in the conception of the subject and assumed its actual existence, and this you merely repeat in the predicate. But if you confess, as every reasonable person must, that every existential proposition is synthetical, how can it be maintained that the predicate of existence cannot be denied without contradiction?—a property which is the characteristic of analytical propositions alone."

Thus, I may cogitate a Being as the highest reality, without defect or imperfection, but the question still remains whether this Being exists or not; for if we wish to predicate the existence of the object of our conception, it must be given through sense, and under the conditions of experience. In the case of a being non-phenomenal this is naturally quite impossible; and "we may as well hope to increase our stock of knowledge by the aid of mere ideas, as a merchant to augment his wealth by the addition of noughts to his cash account."

So much for all Rational Theology. Though certain aspects of Kant's criticism of the Ontological argument have been questioned by philosophers, his arguments are generally accepted as having refuted all proofs of God's existence by reason alone; but, on the other hand, it need scarcely be said that all atheistic contentions are as far as can be seen equally undemonstrable. All we can do in the sphere of Theology, Kant holds, is to recognise that all logical or purely intellectual proofs either for or against God's existence are completely beyond the power of human reason; yet to the moral minded this negative attitude of thought has consolation, in that it leaves open the way for supporting the conviction of God's existence on other grounds. For, as we have seen, the pure Ideal of Reason—the idea of a whole of possible experience which crowns all human knowledge, and makes us pass beyond experience and present to ourselves the Idea of God as a problem to be solved—is there before all attempted proof of the existence of an object corresponding to it; and if, as we shall later find, moral or *practical* reason presupposes or demands the existence of an all-powerful, wise, and good Being as a working postulate, then the Idea, which reason has vainly struggled to support by logic, will be shown to be objectively real. We shall not, it is true, gain a knowledge of God in the sense of knowing Him as an object of experience, but we shall gain all the knowledge required for practical purposes, and Idea of Pure Reason will be realized in that it will have proof of some object corresponding to it. This, however, is the work of later chapters, and does not concern "The Critique of Pure Reason," which is not so much concerned with final philosophical conclusions as with an examination of mind independent of experience, or the study of the principles of synthesis a priori.

CHAPTER IV

THE IDEAS AS REGULATIVE PRINCIPLES

WE have now considered the three Ideas, or the three unities which mind by its very nature is compelled to form when it extends its sphere as far as possible—namely the absolute unity of the thinking self (or the Idea of the Soul), the absolute unity of the series of the conditions of phenomena (or the Idea of a Universe), and the absolute unity of the conditions of all objects of thought in general (or the Idea of God). None of these, as we have seen, will bear the test of criticism; they are only unities projected, so to speak, mere Ideas of the mind, and never constitutive of the real objects they promise. But they are as natural to reason as the categories are to the understanding, and we may depend that whatever is grounded in the nature of our mental powers will have a meaning and purpose which is in harmony with the proper use of those powers.

Thus, the transcendental Ideas have their immanent use, in that they direct the understanding to a certain aim, and as long as they are not mistaken for concepts of real things, and we are not deceived by them, they are useful, indeed necessary,

IDEAS AS REGULATIVE PRINCIPLES 237

to our knowledge ; for just as the categories bring unity into the manifold of sense impressions, so the Ideas of reason bring unity into the manifold concepts of the understanding. The sole purpose of reason, Kant contends, is to arrange our concepts, and to give them that unity which they are capable of possessing when the sphere of their application has been extended as widely as possible. It directs the understanding to a certain aim, the guiding lines towards which all its laws follow, and in which they all meet in one point, so to speak. This point, though a mere imaginary focal point, serves to give to these conceptions the greatest possible unity combined with the greatest possible extension.

To take an example given by Kant, we find in the case of the human mind, feeling, consciousness, imagination, memory, wit, analysis, pleasure, desire, and so on ; and at first we are inclined to assume the existence of just as many different powers as there are different effects. But the very principle of reason desires us to reduce these differences to as small a number as possible, by comparing them and seeking to discover some hidden identity they may have, and so we are soon inquiring whether or not imagination, memory, wit and analysis are not merely different forms of understanding and reason. These relatively fundamental powers must again be compared with each other to discover, if possible, one absolute fundamental power ; and so we go on, creating problems of unity for solution, and pursuing them to a greater unity, the whole process of reason ever advancing to a single point.

This systematic unity, however, is merely logical, says Kant. Reason by its very nature must keep on unifying ; systematic unity is its a priori method. But it is subjectively and logically necessary only, and to infer that it is objectively so is totally without justification. This error is often fallen into in Science, when phenomenal manifestations are reduced to fundamental causes, or powers, or substances ; for in reality such principles are mere Ideas, useful as a hypothetical guide to the solution of problems, but without absolute truth.

The idea that such unity is manifested in nature is always pursued with much ardour by its investigators, who, led on by the transcendental idea of reason, presume that nature is fundamentally unified, no matter how many practical disappointments they meet. Some students of nature (pre-eminently speculative) are intent on the idea of the unity of nature, and are continually seeking to discover likeness in diversity. The diversities of individual things do not exclude identity of the species, the various species are likewise considered as merely different determinations of a few genera, and these again as divisions of still higher orders, and so on. This is the law of homogeneity. Other students of nature (pre-eminently empirical) are more intent on dividing nature into species, and are ever seeking to find the diversity in things. In this way, the law of homogeneity, demanding

IDEAS AS REGULATIVE PRINCIPLES

identity in phenomena, is balanced by another principle—that of species, which requires variety and diversity in things. Thus, every genus has different species; these different sub-species, and so on, Reason always demanding that no species be regarded as the lowest in itself. " This faculty of distinction," says Kant, " acts as a check upon the levity of the former ; and reason exhibits in this respect a double and conflicting interest—on the one hand, the interest in the *extent* (the interest of generality) in relation to genera ; on the other, that of the *content* (the interest of individuality) in relation to the variety of species. In the former case, the understanding cogitates more *under* its conceptions, in the latter it cogitates more *in* them." Kant argues, and gives much evidence to prove, that both these laws are transcendent or regulative ; that is to say, necessary a priori principles of reason guiding our investigations of nature and causing us to think that nature is in conformity with us, or as he puts it, " is purposive to the understanding ".

Moreover, between these two laws and as a means of uniting them, we have the law of the continuity of species, which demands that there be no transition from one species to another by leaps, but only by smaller degrees of differences. In other words, there are no species or sub-species which in the view of reason are the nearest possible to each other ; intermediate species or sub-species are always possible. But this law of continuity, like the other two, is a mere regulative Idea, says Kant.

In experience we can find no object corresponding to it, for in nature the species are actually divided.

Thus, in Kant's words, reason prepares us for the investigation of nature by three principles:— "(1) by the principle of the *homogeneity* of the diverse in higher genera; (2) by the principle of the *variety* of the homogeneous in lower species; and, to complete the systematic unity, it adds (3) a law of the *affinity* of all conceptions, which prescribes a continuous transition from one species to every other by the gradual increase of diversity. We may term these the principles of the *homogeneity*, the *specification*, and the *continuity* of forms." In illustration of the systematic unity produced by these three logical principles, he says:— "Every conception may be regarded as a point, which, as the standpoint of a spectator, has a certain horizon, which may be said to enclose a number of things, that may be viewed, so to speak, from that centre. Within this horizon there must be an infinite number of other points, each of which has its own horizon, smaller and more circumscribed; in other words, every species contains sub-species, according to the principle of specification, and the logical horizon consists of smaller horizons (sub-species), but not of points (individuals), which possess no extent. But different horizons or genera, which include under them so many conceptions, may have one common horizon, from which, as from a mid-point, they may be surveyed; and we may proceed thus, till we arrive at the highest

IDEAS AS REGULATIVE PRINCIPLES

genus, or universal and true horizon, which is determined by the highest conception, and which contains under itself all differences and varieties, as genera, species, and sub-species." To this highest standpoint we are conducted by the law of homogeneity; to all lower and more variously-determined conceptions by the law of specification. "The first law," says Kant, "directs us to avoid the notion that there exist different primal genera, and enounces the fact of perfect homogeneity; the second imposes a check upon this tendency to unite and prescribes the distinction of sub-species before proceeding to apply our general conceptions to individuals. The third unites both the former, by enouncing the fact of homogeneity as existing even in the most various diversity, by means of the gradual translation from one species to another."

THE USE OF THE IDEAS IN EXPERIENCE

Thus, in Kant's view, these three means of investigating nature, are in reality only a priori regulative principles in accordance with which our reason must work, and if we realise this, and never employ them as objective principles, we shall avoid the contradiction which must otherwise inevitably result. Often, he says, we hear men arguing about the distinctive characteristics of men, animals, plants, etc., the one party contending the existence of certain national characteristics, certain well-defined and hereditary distinctions of family, race, and so on; the other party maintaining that nature has endowed all races of men with the same faculties and dispositions, and that all differences are but the result of accidental circumstances. Each believe their judgments rest upon a thorough insight into the subject under discussion, but at bottom, says Kant, each party is unconsciously influenced by the two main regulative Ideas under discussion. The one reasoner is guided entirely by the principle of specification, and is intent on the interest of *diversity;* the other, led on by the principle of homogeneity, is everlastingly seeking to discover *unity*. If only they could each realise this, they would see that there was no reason for warfare, and that each could combine in the furtherance of knowledge by pursuing their investigations under the recognized guidance of the two principles.

In this way, Kant endeavours to show that the three principles have no more objective reality than the three Ideas of the Soul, the Universe, and God; for however far we pursue our investigations, we never find a highest genus, or a lowest species, or an infinite number of intervening species. But they have reality in that they give rules for our understanding to follow, and to renounce them is to renounce reason itself. They keep directing us to look for a highest genus, a lowest species, and so on; and in this way they cause us to extend our experience and bring consistency into the working of our understanding.

The Ideas of pure reason cannot be of themselves

and in their own nature dialectical, says Kant; it is only from their misemployment that fallacies and illusions arise. If only they are regarded as *ideal objects*, and not objects in the *absolute* sense, they can be of great service; for, by investigating nature under the guidance of such ideas, that is to say, under the supposition of such ideal objects, we can bring systematic unity into the empirical employment of our intellignece, and extend our knowledge without ever contradicting it; and, accordingly, it must be a maxim of reason to regulate its procedure according to these Ideas. Thus, the Idea of the soul will guide us in the connection of all psychological phenomena; the Ideas in Cosmology will aid us in discovering the laws of nature; and the Idea of a Supreme Being, as the ground of all possible experience, will help us to organise our entire knowledge. Not, of course, that we must be content to simply deduce psychological phenomena from the soul, or to explain the world-order or systematic unity by God, as if such Ideas had been established as existent objects—this would simply be to substitute an indolent dogmatism for proper scientific inquiry. But if, in our investigations in these various spheres, we keep such Ideas in view, whilst tracing the phenomena from each other in the ordinary scientific way, we shall be provided with a schema which will serve to bring unity into our experience; the supposition of the existence of such ideal objects will furnish regulative principles by which arrangement will be given to the entire field of our scientific knowledge, and accordingly, Kant holds that it must be a maxim of Reason to proceed according to these Ideas. " We must," he says, " in the first place, so connect all the phenomena, actions and feelings of the mind, as if it were a simple substance, which, endowed with personal identity, possesses a permanent existence (in this life at least), while its states, among which those of the body are to be included as external conditions, are in continual change. *Secondly*, in cosmology, we must investigate the conditions of all natural phenomena, internal as well as external, as if they belonged to a chain infinite and without any prime or supreme member, while we do not, on this account, deny the existence of intelligible grounds of these phenomena, although we never employ them to explain phenomena, for the simple reason that they are not objects of our cognition. *Thirdly*, in the sphere of theology, we must regard the whole system of possible experience as forming an absolute, but dependent and sensuously conditioned unity, and at the same time as based upon a sole, supreme, and all-sufficient ground existing apart from the world itself—a ground which is a self-subsistent, primeval and creative reason, in relation to which we so employ our reason in the field of experience, as if all objects drew their origin from that archetype of all reason ".

Thus, as stated before, Kant, whilst advocating the use of the Ideas as regulative principles, particularly emphasises that teleology should on no account

IDEAS AS REGULATIVE PRINCIPLES

be allowed to endanger proper scientific investigation. In psychology, for instance, he does not mean that we should derive the inner phenomena of the mind from a simple soul substance as cause, any more than in theology he means that we should derive the order and the unity of the universe from the Supreme Being. He means derive all psychological phenomena from each other, but in so doing keep before you the Idea that there is unity in this body of phenomena; derive the phenomena of the universe from each other, but use the Idea of a supremely wise ground as a guide to reason in forming rules for the interpretation of the causes and effects discovered. In short, in all cases, we should always proceed in the ordinary scientific manner, tracing causal connections, but in so doing keep before us the Ideas as regulative principles for the purpose of bringing systematic unity into our knowledge.

In this and the foregoing chapters we have explained human knowledge according to Kant's transcendental method. As we have seen, it begins with percepts, passes to concepts, and ends with Ideas. In each of these three elements we have a priori sources of knowledge, but by none of them can we pass beyond experience. The faculty of reason, it is true, deceives us into believing that we can, since it induces us to form Ideas of God, the Universe, and the Soul, and by regarding such Ideas as though they were objects of experience, we are apt to think that we have proved their existence. But a critical examination of the nature of thought in such supposed proof shows that we are here applying categories which have application only to experience to matters which transcend experience, and we see the futility of our efforts. The theological, cosmological, and psychological Ideas can never be constitutive of objects corresponding to them; but our minds are so constituted that we cannot think of systematic unity without giving the Idea some corresponding object, without objectifying it or realizing it, as it were, and we are therefore apt to think there must be real objects corresponding to these Ideas, much as we are led to think that the Ideas of the homogeneity and specification of the forms have objective existence. Such objective existence can never be established; all we can do is to assume such objects problematically, as suppositions, the purpose of which is to guide us in the investigation of experience. We assume God in order that we may have some ground from which and to which to proceed in determining systematic unity. We assume the soul in order to have a ground to which to refer all states of consciousness.

It is clear, however, that though we cannot *establish* the existence of objects corresponding to these Ideas, there is nothing to prevent us from *admitting* its possibility; for, with the exception of the Cosmological Ideas, they are not antinomial; they contain no contradiction. Consequently, no one can establish the non-existence of such objects any more than he can their existence. Further, we *must* admit that such Ideas have a certain comparative reality—namely, "that of the schema of the regulative principle of the systematic unity of all cognition." "They are not," says Kant, "to be regarded as actual things, but as in some measure analogous to them. We abstract from the object of the idea all the conditions which limit the exercise of our understanding, but which, on the other hand, are the sole conditions of our possessing a determinate conception of any given thing. And thus we cogitate a something, of the real nature of which we have not the least conception, but which we represent to ourselves as standing in relation to the whole system of phenomena, analogous to that in which phenomena stand to each other."—" It merely gives us the idea of something, on which the supreme and necessary unity of all experience is based."

PART IV

KANT'S ETHICAL SYSTEM

CHAPTER I

THE PROBLEM OF MORAL FREEDOM

IN "The Critique of Pure Reason" Kant, as we have seen, was mainly concerned with establishing the validity of the principles of science, but this positive work had also a negative aspect, for to prove the validity of such principles was to limit their application to phenomena. In other words, to show the scientific principles valid of objects was to prove that those objects were not things-in-themselves; hence that such principles could not be extended beyond phenomena—a limitation further confirmed by the antinomies into which reason fell when it tried to employ them beyond experience, and which could only be escaped from by recognising the phenomenal nature of the objects with which it was concerned. In this way, "The Critique of Pure Reason," which in science had provided a positive result, in the sphere of metaphysics provided a twofold negative result; whilst it showed that by no effort of reason can God, Freedom, and immortality be established, certain

THE PROBLEM OF MORAL FREEDOM

it was that they can never be refuted. The principles of science have their field of application restricted entirely to empirical knowledge, and the moral and religious consciousness of man is for ever secure from annihilation by such principles, even though it is incapable of proving its convictions theoretically. The ideal demand of reason (the pursuit of the unconditioned) at least shows that, over and above the closed system of nature, there is room for objects, though we cannot determine as real, the thought of which at least shows that phenomena are not real. And thus we may pass from the world of nature and necessity to that of spirit and freedom.

This is as far as the first Critique takes us, but in "The Critique of Practical Reason" Kant deals with another side of human experience, and on practical or moral grounds endeavours to prove what the other Critique had left open. But first we must realise what Kant means by *practical* as opposed to *theoretical* reason, for without this the different Critiques appear independent of each other and lacking in that organic harmony essential to a system of philosophy. Without considering how reason (in relation to which all objects are determined) is conceived by Kant as determining itself, we cannot see how the theories of the second Critique have any relation to those of the first.

Now we have seen how in the phenomenal world everything must be determined by the category of causality; but in self-consciousness there comes a certain exception to this rule. In Kant's words, "Man, who knows all nature besides only through sense, knows himself not only so but through pure apperception and in acts and inner determinations which he cannot reckon among the impressions of sense. He is for himself a phenomenon; but he is also, in view of certain faculties, a purely intelligible object, since the action of such faculties in him cannot be attributed to the receptivity of sense. These faculties we call understanding and reason, the latter of which is properly and pre-eminently distinct from all empirically conditioned powers, as it estimates its objects solely according to Ideas and determines the understanding by these Ideas; while even the understanding itself in experience makes use of conceptions of its own, which, though applicable only to the matter of sense, are pure like the Ideas of reason." In other words, though in theoretical reason man considers himself as an object amongst other objects and therefore as determined, as an acting subject he feels himself to be free, and it is this latter awareness which Kant terms the practical reason. In the phenomenal world all objects are determined by the subject, he tells us, and as object the self is amongst them, but obviously this subject-self that alone determines objects cannot be itself determined. Though when man cognizes himself as object he is certainly a phenomenon, and subject to necessity like all other phenomena, the awareness he has of his actions in pure apperception is a consciousness of a free, active, determining self, and it is this consciousness that Kant means by practical reason. In the process of doing an act I am conscious of being free (practical reason); immediately I make this act an object of my consciousness I appear determined (theoretical reason). This former type of knowledge as opposed to the latter is what Kant deals with in "The Critique of Practical Reason"; he is here making a full consideration of this knowledge of the subject-self we have in acting, particularly in the light that is thrown on it by the moral consciousness. Whereas in "The Critique of Pure Reason" freedom is merely defined negatively in opposition to the necessity in nature, we are now considering it positively in the light of the "I ought" implied in the consciousness of moral responsibility; we leave the system of nature and necessity and pass to the region of spirit and freedom, which science from the very nature of its principles is debarred from entering.

The above will give a rough idea of what Kant means by practical reason; but let us be more explicit, and at the same time we shall be most effectually leading up to Kant's ethical theory. First, what exactly did "The Critique of Pure Reason" demonstrate with respect to freedom and determinism when dealing with the Causal Antinomy? It showed us both sides, it will be remembered, and then reconciled them by transcendental idealism. On the empirical side it showed us that in the world as we know it every phenomenon is conditioned by some other phenomenon ad infinitum; for every effect has its cause, that cause is again only the effect of some prior cause, and however far we pass down the causal chain we shall never find the primal cause. Phenomenally, then, the universe was to be regarded as mechanistic, a clock put together and wound up; and empirically considered man's volitions, like all other phenomena, were simply links in the causal chain. But such a conclusion was so contrary to our sense of moral responsibility that we turned to the other side of the antinomy to see what freedom meant exactly, and we found it to mean a faculty of spontaneously originating a state, the cause of which is not subordinated to another cause determining it in time; that is to say, a state that can begin to act of itself, without any external cause determining it to action according to the law of causality. The problem was thus, whether this freedom or power of self determination could exist along with the certain fact of phenomenal necessity, or whether the necessity found in nature did not entirely exclude it. In other words, did we enounce a contradictory proposition when we said that every effect must have its origin either in nature or in freedom; or was it not possible that both could exist together in the same event in different relations?

The solution to this problem Kant found in his transcendental idealism, it will be remembered. If we conceived phenomena as being reality, then freedom and the necessity in nature were absolutely incompatible; but if, on the contrary, phenomena were held to be nothing more than mere representations connected with each other in accordance with empirical law, then there must be noumena "behind" them, and causality and time not applying to noumena (but being only conditions imposed by our minds), there was no reason why such noumena should not be free, even though phenomena were determined.

The noumenal cause of phenomena Kant called the *intelligible* or non-sensuous cause, in that it was outside space and time; it existed out of and apart from the series of phenomena, yet its effects were to be found in the series of phenomena. Such effects in relation to their intelligible cause might therefore be considered free, though in relation to phenomena they must follow as the direct and determined effect of preceding phenomena; and in this way, if a sensuous object possessed an intelligible or non-sensuous faculty by which it could initiate phenomena, the causality of such an object might be regarded from two different points of view. As regards the cause of its action which is noumenal, it might be considered to be intelligible; as regards its effects, which become part of the phenomenal world, it *might* be regarded as sensuous. Accordingly we had to form both an intelligible and empirical conception of the causality of such a faculty, both, however, having reference to the same effect. The one might be regarded as the object's character as thing-in-itself, the latter its character as a phenomenon.

Now in its character as thing-in-itself, such a subject would not be subordinate to the conditions of time, Kant explained, time being only a condition of phenomena; no actions of this subject would *begin* or *cease to be*, so it would be free from the law of change, by which everything which happens must have a cause in the preceding phenomena. Thus, it would *determine and not be determined*. Again, this intelligible character would not be cognized, because we can perceive nothing but phenomena; yet, on the other hand, its character as phenomena would fall in line with the law of causality and would appear to follow as the result of the preceding phenomena, thus being phenomenally determined. In this way nature and freedom, understood critically, could exist without contradiction in the same event.

Applying this doctrine to man, then, we saw that though every action phenomenally considered must be connected with an empirical cause, it was perfectly possible that this empirical causality might itself be the effect of a non-empirical and intelligible causality—its connection with the natural causes remaining nevertheless unbroken. Man was to be regarded as an intelligible being, Kant contended, and to this intelligible element in his nature the sense forms did not apply; hence, though it was true that in human action, as in everything else, one phenomenon must certainly appear the cause of the other phenomenon considered empirically, yet the real cause of the causal phenomenon might quite conceivably be reason, pure thought, which was self originated and not caused by other phenomena, though it must always appear to be. Thus, on the one hand, man was a phenomenon of the sensuous world and therefore a link in the causal chain; but, on the other, he was an intelligible being, himself initiating the empirical cause which constitutes a link in such chain. He cognized himself not only by his senses (as phenomenon), but also through pure apperception, and in respect of this latter he knew himself to be an intelligible object—intelligible because his actions cannot be ascribed to sensuous receptivity.

Negative Freedom Made Positive by the Moral Law

In this way Kant, in "The Critique of Pure Reason," showed at least the possibility of free will, in that transcendental freedom is at any rate perfectly compatible with natural necessity. For human beings there are two selves—the object self known empirically through the senses and therefore determined like all other objects, and the subject self known through pure apperception and in relation to which alone are phenomena determined. The object self is similar to other objects in the empirical world; it is determined in all its states and changes in relation to other objects; it can only act on them as they can on it, and such respective actions and reactions are determined by universal laws. But the subject self, which originates actions, is very different; for it is in relation to this self only that objects are determined, and it would therefore be absurd to regard this self as itself determined. Accordingly, in this knowledge of himself as active determining subject man must be in closer touch with reality than in any knowledge he gains through the senses. In the process of originating a free act he is part of the spiritual world; hence it is not surprising to find Kant associating this subject self in its active determining capacity with the moral law and the consciousness of ourselves as free agents which it necessarily involves, and telling us that the freedom of the will, which "The Critique of Pure Reason" showed to be possible, becomes guaranteed a positive fact by the moral law within us. "That reason has causality," says Kant, "or at least that we represent it as having such causality, is clear from the imperatives which in all our practical life we set up as rules for our executive powers. The *ought* expresses a kind of necessity, a kind of connection of actions with their grounds or reasons, such as to be found nowhere else in the whole natural world. For, of the natural world our understanding can know nothing except what is, what has been, or what will be. We cannot say that in it anything *ought to be* other than in fact it was, is, or will be. In fact, so long as we are considering merely the course of nature, the 'ought' has absolutely no meaning. We can as little inquire what *ought* to happen in nature, as we can inquire what properties a circle ought to have. In the former case, we are limited to the question what actually happens, just as, in the latter case, we are limited to the questions what properties the figure in question actually has. Now this ' ought ', in fact, expresses a possible action of which the ground is nothing but a conception ; while of an action which is a mere natural event the ground must always be a phenomenon. It is true, indeed, that no action can be required of us as a duty which is not possible under natural conditions ; but these natural conditions do not relate to the determination of the will, but only to the effect or consequence thereof in the phenomenal world. Let there be ever so many natural grounds which urge me to an act of will, ever so many sensuous stimuli, yet they cannot make an act one that *ought to be.* The will they can produce will have only a conditioned, not an absolute necessity, against which reason opposes the ' ought ' as that which prescribes to it measure and end, or even absolutely and authoritatively prohibits it. Be it an object of mere sensuous desire (the pleasant), or be it an object of pure reason (the good), what we have to note is, that reason never yields to that ground which is empirically given, that it never follows the order of things as they present themselves in the phenomenal world, but *with perfect spontaneity creates for itself an order of its own according to ideas,* into which it fits the empiric conditions, and according to which it declares actions to be necessary which have not taken place, and which perhaps will never take place. All these actions, therefore, without any regard to the actual event, it presupposes that reason is capable of realising ; for if it did not do so, it would not expect any effect of its ideas in the world of experience."

It may be said that, just as in " The Critique of Pure Reason " Kant had been concerned with the distinction and opposition between empirical and a priori knowledge, so in "The Critique of Practical Reason " he is concerned with the opposition between sensuous propensity and the law of reason ; it is an opposition between the self as object determined by other objects, and the conscious self as subject that determines itself. On the one hand, we have the motives of passion, derived from the self's objective and phenomenal existence ; on the other, the motives which the conscious subject derives from its own being. The former, as they represent themselves in opposition to the latter (in opposition, that is to say, to the motive which the rational being derives from his own moral nature), are recognised as motives which *ought not* to determine man except in so far as they coincide with the motive of reason ; whilst the latter, in opposition to passion, appears as a " categorical imperative " with a feeling of moral necessity to exclude such passions from determining our will.

In so far as passion does influence a rational being it is only in so far as it is taken up or subsumed under the motive of reason : we are never, says Kant, fatally determined by it. But how we can unite the consciousness of rational self determination with determination by passion Kant does not explain, though he thinks he can explain why. He considers the matter inexplicable because of the two different views we have of the self—on the one hand, as a phenomenal object, on the other, as noumenon. I can look at myself as a noumenon, abstracting the conditions of space and time which make me phenomenally determined, but I can never unite the two orders. I may determine myself in accordance with the moral ideal, but I can never find myself so determined as an empirical fact. Though an action may be a complete self-determination of the will, it can only be expressed in phenomenal terms and must thus appear determined ; for the natural system is the only system we know under laws, and we are thus compelled to use it when we think of the realisation of the moral law. But this inability of ours in no way excludes the transcendental reality of the moral law. On the contrary, the moral law, with its absolute imperative, turns the idea of freedom into an actuality or fact of reason, and convinces us of the reality of the noumenal as against the phenomenal. We are compelled to conceive ourselves as members of the intelligible world in order to think of ourselves as free, and we are compelled to think of ourselves as free because we are obliged to think of ourselves as subjected to the moral law.

The moral law, in fact, forces us to think of ourselves as noumenal self-determining beings; and this being so, the impossibility of representing ourselves as free need not worry us, since our knowledge, limited as it is to the phenomenal, must of necessity find such a representation impossible. We can see how even theoretically transcendental freedom is quite consistent with phenomenal determinism; in the consciousness of the subject self we have in action we recognise ourselves to be self determining, and not as forced to action by sensuous motives. Accordingly, though we cannot explain *how* we are free, any more than we can explain positively the nature of noumena, we recognise that we are so; for not only is freedom assured by the moral law, but it has been proved that phenomena are only determined in relation to the self, and it would be absurd to regard this self which alone does the determining as itself determined.

CHAPTER II

THE FORMULATION OF THE MORAL LAW

HAVING seen how Kant prepares the way for his moral system by making a very strong case for the freedom of the will, without which all morality (in the religious sense at least) becomes impossible, let us now proceed to his formulation of the moral law. By many this has been much criticised, and it has been pointed out that, by abstracting all motives of self interest, on the one hand, and denying the moral value of sympathy, on the other, Kant has placed undue restrictions on human nature. But it must not be forgotten that the greatest necessity in morality is to exclude from it all egoistic motives and all maudlin sentiment, and no moral system is so strict in this respect as Kant's. It may be said at once that, however abstract the system may be, it represents one of the strongest answers to Hedonism that has ever been put forward, and that, too, at a stage where the antagonism between the Hedonists and those supporting the theory of duty for duty's sake has reached its ultimate form. To quote Caird, " We have in Kant's ethical works the final and most explicit expression of a view of the moral life which, in some form or other, has held the balance with Hedonism throughout the whole history of ethical philosophy. In dealing with Kant we are considering a vital opposition which has affected the whole history of Ethics, and in which, therefore, we may suppose each side to represent a real interest of the moral life. Though Kant may be classed as belonging to one of the contending parties, and though he expresses the negative view of the moral life in its relation to sense and passion in no hesitating terms, yet he has continually present to him the necessity of a reconciliation, and he has put the case on behalf of his one-sided theory in such a way as to show conclusively all its strength and all its weakness."

In his first ethical work, "The Metaphysic of Ethics", Kant, in defining the good, takes his stand on the ordinary moral consciousness, and by making a thorough analysis of it and excluding particularly all that it does not imply, endeavours to reach the quintessence of all morals. By this method, supported in "The Critique of Practical Reason" by additional methods, he reaches the conception that there is nothing absolutely good save only a good will. We do not, he says, call a man good because of his talents or his wealth, or even because of his firmness of resolution, his abstinence or his self command : a man may have all these and use them for evil ends ; indeed, it is quite possible to conceive a man with the brains of a Newton, the resolution of a Napoleon, and the moderation and self command of the perfect Puritan, who is yet nothing but a selfish tyrant upsetting the whole world and doing so all the more effectually on account of these qualities. Likewise, we do not, on the other hand, call a man good because he produces beneficial effects in the world; for men often produce beneficial effects when acting on the lowest motives—as, for instance, the greedy capitalist who enlivens trade, or the social reformer actuated by nothing but self display. No; we call a man good because of the worth of his volition, because of his self determined desire and persistent efforts to bring about good ends; and no matter how stupid a man may be in carrying his wishes into practice, if only they are noble and benevolent, and he lives an arduous life in trying to bring them about, we concede to him the highest place in the moral kingdom. In this way, Kant concludes that it is the good will, and the good will alone, that constitutes the moral worth of a man.

But what precisely constitutes the good will? Kant answers that this can only be found by analysing the idea of duty, and here, again, our best method of reaching the quintessence of what duty involves will be to eliminate all that it does not involve. Thus, guided by the average man's consciousness of duty, it is perfectly clear that good actions done with ulterior motives are not acts of duty; to be honest on the conviction that honesty is the best policy is only making a bad will worse by associating with it a wisdom that ought to enable me to recognise the action's moral worthlessness. And again, actions done because they are the spontaneous outcome of my nature are scarcely consistent with the idea of duty : if, for instance, I am enjoying life immensely, it is no act of duty on my part to refrain from committing suicide, nor, similarly, can I be conscious of great military duty if, being a man who naturally loves a fight, I join in the first war that presents itself and throw myself into the thick of it purely for the excitement. The sense of duty always involves the overcoming of some obstacle in my nature recognised to be bad, and the dutiful man, even if he gets to a stage where he is for the most part good, always recognises that he has still something further to overcome in order to realise his ideal. Hence Kant concludes that duty " involves the idea of a good will under certain limitations ", or an action done through the consciousness of its being a better action than the natural opposing tendency.

From the above, then, we conclude that an action has moral worth only so far as it is done in obedience to duty, and that even if it does not attain its end, provided every effort in the agent's power is made to attain it, its moral value is unimpaired ; whilst, on the contrary, even if an act is instrumental in producing good, it has no moral value unless actuated by the motive of duty. Accordingly, Kant says duty may be defined as " the necessity of an act as motivated solely by

FORMULATION OF THE MORAL LAW

reverence for the law ", and reverence, he states, can be felt for nothing else. I cannot feel reverence, on the one hand, for a good action done out of natural desire without any sense of duty, for I cannot feel it a self determination; nor can I, on the other hand, feel reverence for mere effects without they have been actuated by consciousness of duty. Consequently there is only one thing that I can feel reverence for, only one thing that I can regard as truly moral, and that is the moral law itself, the bare idea of duty. " As I have deprived the will of all motives which might arise for it out of the following of any special law, there remains nothing but the universal accordance of the action with law to serve for a principle to actuate the will, i.e., I am required to act only in such a way *that I can will that my maxim* (or subjective principle of action) *should become a universal law.*" This command Kant holds to be the quintessence of the moral consciousness; it is all that is left after we have abstracted all that the moral consciousness obviously does not imply. It is in the seat of practical reason itself, and the average man, however little he may be conscious of it and however lacking he may be in the far-sightedness required to act in accordance with honesty being the best policy, finds himself intuitively recognising the law as soon as he comes to form any practical decision. In Kant words, it is part of that " obscurely thought metaphysic which dwells with every man as part of his rational capacity."

In his subsequent ethical work, "The Critique of Practical Reason", Kant reaches the same conclusion. Here we have, as it were, a struggle between the sensuous propensity of man and the law of reason already alluded to. On the one side, are the ends to which desire may be directed, all empirical since they are all in some way or other concerned with the *matter* of consciousness; on the other, is the law of reason, or reason acting on a motive derived entirely from itself, which constitutes a moral law of a universal order. The former are to be regarded as furnishing sensuous and egoistic motives for the will, and are all of the same principle of self love; but, according to the testimony of our moral consciousness, this principle is directly opposed to the principle of morality, says Kant. The principle of morality is to be found only in the pure (a priori) form of reason, which prescribes for the will a universal law such as no empirical principle can give; namely, a categorical imperative, which, expressed in the form of a natural law, gives the command : *Act so that the maxim of thy will can at the same time be acceptable as the principle of a universal legislation.* Man, being both a sensuous and a rational being, and the senses being in constant opposition to reason, this fundamental law of practical reason bears the form of a command, and consciousness of this command is a fact of reason. " While all material eudemonistic principles flow from the heteronomy of arbitrary unregulated choice, the command of reason flows from the autonomy of the will. Man in his character as a rational being or a noumenon gives law to himself as a sensuous being or a phenomenon."

It will be seen how Kant arrives at his categorical imperative in "The Critique of Practical Reason" by setting out more explicitly this struggle between man's sensuous propensity and the law of reason, and taking particular care to note how he separates the empirical and a priori factors as they influence our willing. Here Kant first of all draws a distinction between, on the one hand, all promptings to the will by passion, and, on the other, the practical *law* of reason, i.e. reason acting on a motive derived entirely from itself. He reaches the categorical imperative by three theorems. The first theorem is that "all practical principles which presuppose an object (a matter) of desire as a ground of determination for the will are empirical, and can yield no practical law." And by this Kant means that in order that the idea of an object should be a ground of action, it must affect our sensibility in a particular way, i.e., it must either give pleasure or pain, and no motive of this type can express a practical law of a universal nature; for it is empirical and not a priori, and cannot, therefore, set before the subject a ground of determination that holds good in all cases and for all rational beings. Here the rational being does not determine an object as desirable and so awake in himself a desire for it, but waits for the object to determine him from without, and in accordance with whether it gives pleasure or pain it becomes a maxim influencing his will. It is therefore clear that such empirical maxims are all the seeking of pleasure or the avoidance of pain ; and so there follows the second theorem : " all material practical principles as such are of one and the same kind, and fall under the universal principle of self-love or our own happiness." By happiness Kant understands " a consciousness on the part of a rational being of the agreeableness of life, accompanying without interruption his entire existence " ; and in his view there is no justification in this respect for drawing a line between different kinds of desires in accordance with whether they have their origin from the pleasures of sense or of understanding. It is one and the same vital force expressing itself in all desires ; they all presuppose objects of some kind or other, and all fall under the same principle of self love, or the pursuit of our own pleasure. Now it is true that the idea of happiness furnishes a kind of unity under which the various objects of desire may be brought, but such a principle can never be regarded as constituting a universal principle of the type implied in moral action. Happiness is one thing for one person, another for another, and is subject to changes even with the same person ; hence it can never provide the necessity of a law, which Kant holds can only be based on a priori grounds. Thus, we see that (theorem 1) nothing empirical can give a universal practical law, that (theorem 2) every concrete object of the will which serves as a motive *is* empirical; and from this follows the third theorem: "that if a rational being is to think of his maxims as universal practical laws, he must think of them as principles which contain the determining ground of the will only as respects its form and not as respects its matter." In other words, "when we separate from a law all its matter, i.e. every object of will which can determine it, nothing remains but the mere form of a universal legislation. Hence a rational being cannot think of his principles of action as constituting universal laws unless he assumes that it is the mere form of these maxims, according to which they are fitted to be elements in a universal legislation, that by itself makes them into such practical laws." Moral action is reason acting on a motive derived entirely from itself, in opposition to the motives of passion relating to external objects. After every such motive of passion has been set aside, nothing remains but the pure form of universality with which reason invests every matter that is brought to it. And in this way we again reach the categorical imperative reached by analysis of the ordinary moral consciousness in "The Metaphysic of Ethics", and which, when translated into terms of our understanding, may be expressed as, *Act so that the maxim of thy will can at the same time be acceptable as the principle of a universal legislation.* This imperative, Kant contends, is the only practical law we can conceive of as a universal law; and it not only corresponds correctly with our moral consciousness, but is the moral law obedience to which can give the best practical effects. It is not a hypothetical maxim; it does not say, "Do this, if you would be successful, healthy, or obtain reward in the next world." It is categorical; its command, saying, "Do it because it is your duty to do it and for no other reason", and in this way we recognise it as absolute and not merely relative.

Application of the Moral Law

Kant next proceeds to the application of this imperative as a criterion of the morality of acts in life, but before doing so he reminds us that when we express the law as "Act so that the maxim of thy will can at the same time be acceptable as the principle of a universal legislation", we are not expressing the moral law itself, but are only translating the moral law into a law of nature, because this is the only way in which we can think of it as realised. Consequently we must always remember that "this comparison of the maxim of our actions with a universal law of nature is not the motive which is to determine our will to perform them", but the law of nature serves as a type for our judgment, and if any action is not of such a type that it can stand the test of this law, it is morally wrong. Kant divides duties into those of perfect and imperfect obligation. He attempts to show that when we commit breaches of these,

FORMULATION OF THE MORAL LAW

we find, on applying our moral law, that we are at once in difficulties; for in breaches of duties of perfect obligation we are involved in a direct contradiction whenever we think of such breaches as universal laws, and in duties of imperfect obligation, though there is no such direct contradiction in their breaches, yet a rational being, on willing that the maxims of such acts should be universalised, is divided against himself. To deal first with breaches of duties of perfect obligation, we may take the case of the man who borrows money under a lying pretence to pay back. If such a man translates his lying pretence into a universal law of nature, he sees at once that " the universality of a law according to which each one, when he believes himself to be in need, may promise whatever he pleases with the resolve not to keep his promise, would make impossible the promising and any end it could have in view; since no one under such a system would consider that anything *was* promised to him, but would laugh at all such utterances as mere silly show and hypocrisy."

An example of a breach of the duties of imperfect obligation is the case of a man who, being well off, is totally indifferent to taking any trouble to assist anyone else. Let such a man put his conduct to the test by conceiving the principle of his action as the universal law, and what is the result? He finds that, though men might still exist on such a principle, it is impossible for him to will that such principle should become a universalised law. "For a will which so determined would contradict itself, since many cases may occur in which the individual needs the love and sympathy of others, in which, by such a natural law springing from his own will, he would absolutely deprive himself of all hope of assistance." Thus, in the case of breaches of duty of perfect obligation we cannot even think of them as universalised without contradiction; and in breaches of duties of imperfect obligation, though we can think of them as universalised, we can never will them to become so, for such a will would contradict itself. It becomes clear that what we really want in all such cases is that the law remain in force for the rest of the world, but an exception to be made in it in our own favour; and, applying the universal test to such willing, this again would involve a contradiction.

So much for the first formula of the moral law, but a careful consideration of all said before about the nature of the law shows that other formulæ are needed before the law is adequately expressed in such forms as will guide us in carrying it into effect. First, in morality we have, according to Kant, to do with a being "possessed of a faculty of determining itself according to the consciousness of certain laws"; these laws are conditions of the being's existence; hence we are concerned with a rational being making its own end, or determining itself by its own nature. Such laws, then, must be regarded as having unconditioned authority;

they are ends in themselves; and a rational being therefore cannot be regarded as *a means* to some other end. The man who places money and power before all else no doubt feels that the object of his desire is an end in itself, and that he himself and all others he can get under him are only means to this end; but a brief consideration of the matter will show the short-sightedness of such a view. For, as Kant says, " No object of desire has more than a conditional value; for if the desires and the wants based on them did not exist, their objects would be without value." Likewise " the desires themselves as sources of such wants, cannot claim any absolute value such as should cause them to be in themselves objects of desire," for they are only means to ends. Hence the value of every object that can be acquired by our actions is only a conditional value; they have only a relative value as a means, and are therefore called *things;* while rational beings are called *persons*, " because their nature already marks them out as ends in themselves, i.e., as beings who ought never to be used merely as means. Such beings are objects of reverence. They are not subjective ends, whose existence, as an effect of our action, has a value *for us*, but *objective ends*, i.e., beings whose existence is an end in itself, an end for which no other end can be substituted so as to reduce it to the position of means. Apart from such beings, indeed, we could find nothing of *absolute value* anywhere, and in the absence of all but conditional and accidental ends there could be no highest practical principle for the reason."

From this follows a second formula for the categorical imperative: "Always treat humanity, both in your own person and in the persons of others, as an end and never merely as a means." And if we take the examples of breaches of duties of perfect and imperfect obligation used before, we shall see the inconsistency with the formula they involve. If, for instance, I make a deceitful promise to a man, I am obviously using him as a means without at the same time treating him as an end in himself; and as regards my never troubling to assist others, though such conduct may not be inconsistent with the mere maintenance of the existence of humanity, it would at least be inconsistent with the positive furtherance of such an end. "Such positive agreement would involve that each should seek, so far as lies in him, to further the ends of the others. For if a conscious subject be an end in himself, and if the conception of him as such is to produce its full effect in me, his ends must, so far as possible, become also my ends."

Thus, the first formula "expresses the idea that the moral law is not only universal, but that its essence lies in the form of universality"; the second tells us "that the consciousness of that law is one with that consciousness of himself as an end which belongs to the rational being as such." By uniting these two points we therefore get the idea that the rational being is subject to a law which, though universal, is nevertheless enacted by himself; and from this Kant draws the third formula of the law: " Act in conformity with the idea that the will of every rational being is a universally legislative will." Here we have the idea of " a Kingdom of ends ", a society of beings each of which is an end in itself and a means to the end of others. Whilst man has to submit to certain laws, in so doing he is only submitting to himself, for he himself originates and determines these laws. This is Kant's principle of the Autonomy of the will; the same individual who, as rational, lays down the law, as a sensitive being is subject to it. In Kant's words, " the conception that every rational being must contemplate himself through all the maxims of his will as universally legislative, in order from this point of view to judge himself and his actions, leads to another closely connected and very fruitful conception, viz., to the conception of a kingdom of ends. By a Kingdom, I here mean the systematic combination of a number of diverse rational beings under common laws. Now, such laws will determine the ends of the rational beings in question, so far as they are universally valid ends. Hence, when we abstract from all personal differences of rational beings, and likewise all the content of their private ends, we get the idea of a complete and systematically connected whole of all ends (a whole of rational beings as ends in themselves, as well as of the special ends which each of them may set up for himself), i.e., a kingdom of ends such as is possible according to the principles already laid down. To this kingdom of ends every rational being belongs as a *member*, who, though universally legislative, is yet submitted to the laws he enacts. At the same time, he belongs to it also as a *sovereign*, because as legislative he is submitted to no will but his own. The rational being must always regard himself as legislative, in a kingdom of ends which is made possible by the freedom of the will."

From the above it will be seen that, according to Kant, all moral conduct, whether in relation to self or to others as members of a Kingdom of ends, arises from a law which man imposes upon himself as a rational being and which he recognises as an unconditional command alone having absolute worth. Morality is a struggle in which man has to limit the pleasures derived from satisfying his sensuous propensity so as to bring them into conformity with the law of reason. On the one hand, are the motives based upon feelings of pleasure and pain, dependent on the action of objects on our sensibility ; on the other, the motives which are derived from the consciousness of ourselves as rational subjects. Associated with these latter is a consciousness of freedom, in that we are conscious of being able to overcome the motives of desire, and to regard ourselves as capable of determination by the unconditioned imperative of duty. Moral feeling may therefore be described as, on the one side, negative and painful, on the other, positive and elevating. Whilst conformity to morality produces a painful or at least negative effect on our sensibility in that it curbs the movement of natural desire, in the consciousness of obeying a law arising from our rational nature there is intellectual elevation. Our self love and natural inclination to be satisfied with ourselves is set aside, and we realise that the pursuit of our own happiness except so far as it be limited to conditions of agreement with the law is of no moral value or merit. We find that "what humiliates us on the sensuous side, on the intellectual side elevates us." "The soul believes itself to be exalted, just in the measure in which it recognises the elevation of the holy law above itself and the frailty of its own nature."

The feeling accompanying moral action can therefore be described neither as pleasure nor pain; it is rather a positive feeling reached through negative—a limitation of sensuous pleasure which leads to the exaltation of conscious unison with a higher law disinterestedly obeyed. According to Kant, reverence for the law and for those who have realised it is the essence of the feeling, and this is as far as a man can go. The idea of the perfect love that casteth out fear he regards as a dangerous principle, since if man tries to rise above reverence, he will inevitably fall beneath it; for by changing reverence into love he will only be making himself influenced by an object to which he is attracted by desire, instead of acting in obedience to the law by which alone he is free. The characteristic grade of moral life which man should endeavour to maintain is *virtue*, a goodness that continually maintains itself in effort and conflict, and not an extravagant attempt to act with magnanimous and lofty exaltation, which causes him to plume himself on his merits. The Christian command to love God above all and our neighbour as ourselves is the best maxim, Kant contends. " Love to God as an inclination (pathological love) is impossible, for God is no object of sense ; and love to man, though possible, cannot be imperative ; for it is impossible to love another merely at command. It is, therefore, *practical love* that is meant in that kernel of all laws. To love God is gladly to obey His commands ; to love our neighbour is gladly to do all our duties to him. But the law that makes this our rule of action cannot be a command to *have* this temper of mind in acting, but only to *strive* after it : a command to do something gladly would be a contradiction. The Christian principle is, therefore, to be regarded as setting the true moral habit of mind before us as an ideal of perfection which can be attained by no created being ; though it is the antitype to which we should endeavour to assimilate ourselves in an uninterrupted but endless progress."

CHAPTER III

KANT'S MORAL THEOLOGY

KANT'S ethical theory forms an integral part of his philosophy, for it is in the requirements of moral reason that he finds the necessity for conceiving the reality of the three Ideas of pure reason that the first Critique held to be undemonstrable. We have seen how the freedom of the will, in "The Critique of Pure Reason" merely shown to be possible, in "The Critique of Practical Reason" is converted into a positive conception by the " I ought " of moral consciousness. In the same way, says Kant, when we understand the moral law fully and see all that is demanded by it, so the Ideas of God and of the soul become similarly established, for it becomes impossible to conceive the law we are commanded to fulfil as possible of being fulfilled unless we conceive God and immortality as being actual.

He argues thus :—the categorical imperative commands an absolutely good will, a virtuous will, a holy will. It is the essence of our moral consciousness that the ideal of complete good should ultimately be attainable, and we can only conceive the complete good as the union of virtue and happiness; for that a creature should have a need of happiness, should deserve it, and never attain it, cannot be consistent with our idea of justice. Complete good, then, involves the combination of perfect virtue with perfect happiness, and in the progress towards this ideal we are compelled to conceive the latter following in proportion to the former. But here two difficulties meet us—first, the possibility of the realisation of perfect virtue in a being constituted as man; and, second, as to the combination of happiness and virtue. With regard to the first, we certainly have to conceive the possibility of perfectly realising virtue; for the categorical imperative implies it, since complete virtue is commanded by it, and a command that could not be realised would be meaningless. But man is a sensuous being, full of selfish motives, and it seems impossible that in this existence the law of reason should be his sole actuating motive to the exclusion of all influence of desire. The difficulty is to be solved only by the idea of a *progressus ad infinitum*, in which the sensuous nature is continuously triumphed over by the moral. An eternal progress towards perfection is necessary; hence, in accordance with our moral reason, we must conceive the soul to be immortal. In Kant's own words, "the perfect accordance of the will with the moral law is holiness, a perfection of which no rational being of the sensible world is capable at any moment of his existence. Since, nevertheless, it is required as practically necessary, it can only be found in a *progress in infinitum* towards that perfect accordance, and on the principles of pure practical reason it is necessary to assume such a practical progress as the real object of our will. Now this endless progress is only possible on the supposition of an endless duration of the existence and personality of the same rational being (which is called the immortality of the soul). The summum bonum then practically is only possible on the supposition of the immortality of the soul; consequently this immortality being inseparably connected with the moral law is a Postulate of pure practical reason."

As far as the second difficulty is concerned, the combination of happiness and virtue, it is clear that the idea of complete good which the moral law commands must involve the union of happiness with virtue in just proportion; but the question arises, How can such a union be actually realised? An examination of the matter will show that we here have two completely different principles to harmonise, and neither a mechanistic nature, on the one hand, nor man's power of moral determination, on the other, can possibly reconcile them. For man happiness means that everything in the world goes according to his wish and will; it is the harmony of physical nature with his whole end, inclusive of his power of self determination as a moral agent. But the very essence of free self determination in accordance with the moral law is that it should be independent of the mechanism of nature ; and thus, if virtue and happiness are to be combined, we have to unite, on the one hand, the mechanism of nature which is quite independent of man's power of self determination, and, on the other, man's self determination as a moral agent, the very essence of which is that it should be independent of the mechanism of nature. Such a combination appears impossible, but if the conception of complete good is to be realised, and if the ultimate purpose of the world is a union of perfect virtue and perfect happiness, as the moral law demands, it has to be made. To bring about the combination it becomes necessary that nature should be so constructed that it should be converging, as it were, to man's moral ends ; that nature and the moral law should be in conformity ; and this involves that there must be a Being quite distinct from nature, but at the same time its cause, who has combined the laws of nature with the moral law. Now before such a Being could bring about such a combination, before, that is to say, nature could be constructed as to comply with the conscious moral ends of man, it would be necessary that there should be a consciousness of such moral ends, and since consciousness of laws implies a *rational* being and decision in accordance with laws implies a *will*, it follows that the supreme ground of nature is a Being who has acted with intelligence and will, or in other words, God. Thus, the conception of the *highest derived good*, the idea that the great purpose of the universe is the ultimate combination of perfect virtue and perfect happiness (as man's moral consciousness inclines him to think), necessarily implies *the highest original Good*, the existence of a Being who has created the world with consciousness of and in accordance with the ultimate moral end. If the idea of complete good is to be attained, as the moral law leads us to believe, it becomes not only possible but necessary to postulate the existence of God. We are thus led to teleology and God by the moral law.

To ensure an accurate statement of this " faith of reason ", as Kant calls it, it is perhaps as well to quote Kant's own words. " Happiness," he says, " is the condition of a rational being in the world with whom everything goes according to his wish and will; it rests therefore on the harmony of physical nature with his whole end, and likewise with the essential determining principle of his will. Now the moral law as a law of freedom commands by determining principles which ought to be quite independent on nature and on its harmony with our faculty of desire (as springs). But the acting rational being in the world is not the cause of the world and of nature itself. There is not the least ground therefore in the moral law for a necessary connexion between morality and proportionate happiness in a being that belongs to the world as part of it, and therefore dependent on it, and which for that reason cannot by his will be a cause of this nature, nor by his own power make it thoroughly harmonise, as far as his happiness is concerned, with his practical principles. Nevertheless, in the practical problem of pure reason, i.e., the necessary pursuit of the *summum bonum*, such a connexion is postulated as necessary : we ought to endeavour to promote the *summum bonum*, which therefore must be possible. Accordingly, the existence of a cause of all nature, distinct from nature itself and containing the principle of this connexion, namely, of the exact harmony of happiness with morality is also *postulated*. Now this supreme cause must contain the principle of the harmony of nature and not merely with a law of the will of rational beings, but with the conception of this law in so far as they make it the supreme determining principle of the will, and consequently not merely with the form of morals, but with their morality as their motive, that is, with their moral character. Therefore the *summum bonum* is possible in the world only on the supposition of a supreme Nature having a causality corresponding to moral character. Now a being that is capable of acting on the conception of laws is an *intelligence* (a rational being), and the causality of such a being according to this conception of laws is his *will* ; therefore the supreme cause of nature, which must be presupposed as a condition of the *summum bonum*, is a being which is the cause of nature by *intelligence* and *will*, consequently its author, that is God. It follows that the postulate of the possibility of the *highest derived good* (the best world) is likewise the postulate of the reality of the *highest original good*, that is to say, of the existence of God. Now it was seen to be a duty for us to promote the *summum bonum*, consequently it is not merely allowable but is a necessity connected with duty as a requisite, that we should presuppose the possibility of the *summum bonum*, and as this is possible only on condition of the existence of God, it inseparably connects the supposition of this with duty, that is, it is morally necessary to assume the existence of God."

Thus, the moral law, demanding as it does the conception of the *summum bonum* as the ultimate goal of humanity, finally leads to religion; for it becomes necessary to postulate God as the Being who has so united nature and morality as to make the *summum bonum* possible, and this means that God has created the world with an ultimate moral purpose. Man, in acting morally, is therefore fulfilling God's will; he is forced to recognise all duties as divine commands—commands of a morally perfect, all-powerful Being. But, though in acting morally man is in harmony with God's will, it is clear that he must not act so merely *because* of his belief in God; for we have no way of arriving at a knowledge of God except through morality, and to make our morality dependent on our knowledge of God would be not only to put the cart before the horse, but to destroy the very meaning of morality by making it nothing more than the outcome of fear or the hope of reward. Thus, in this moral theology, there can be no selfish motive to goodness; no fear, on the one hand, or hope of reward, on the other. Goodness is simply acting in accordance with the disinterested command of the moral self, which alone enables us to form the conception of the *summum bonum*. Such conception next leads to God—in that it is necessary to postulate a being who has created the world in accordance with this conception and who will proportion happiness in accordance with virtue—and it is true that I then realise that it is God's will that I should act morally, and that in attempting to promote the *summum bonum* I am incidentally promoting my own happiness; but in the whole development of this theology the idea of my own happiness necessarily comes last of all, and fear of God and hope of reward can play no part in my conduct in such a religion. In a word, its essence is not that I should strive ultimately to gain happiness, but that I should strive to become worthy of happiness. Hence, if it be asked, as it often is, What is God's purpose in creating the world? we must not reply the happiness of the rational beings in it, or even their goodness, but the *summum bonum*; for our only knowledge of the highest original good is our conception of the highest derived good, and we could not think of God as all good and all wise unless His wishes were not only our happiness but our goodness. The ultimate end of creation is best expressed as the glory of God, says Kant, meaning by those words, not the desire to be praised, but complete obedience to His Holy Law, crowned by a corresponding happiness.

This moral theology, bears a close resemblance to the philosophy of Christianity, so Kant tells us, for both base immortality and God on similar grounds. In Christianity the moral law is holy (unvielding), and demands holiness of morals, but man has a constant propensity to transgression, and the most he can attain to is only virtue, a dutiful disposition arising from respect for the law. The holiness which the Christian law requires is therefore only possible on the condition of a progress *in infinitum*, and for this reason justifies man in hoping for an endless duration of his existence. Again, the ultimate unity of virtue and happiness is based on very similar ideas as is the postulate of God in the Kantian moral system. In Christianity the worth of a character perfectly in accord with the moral law is infinite, and the only hindrance to all possible happiness to humanity is lack of morality. But the moral law itself does not promise happiness, and in this world there is no necessary connection between morality and happiness; therefore Christianity supplies this defect by representing the world in which rational beings devote themselves with all their soul to the moral law as a *Kingdom of God*, in which nature and morality are brought into harmony foreign to each by a holy Author, who thereby makes the conception of the *summum bonum* possible. In this life the Christian must strive towards holiness, but the bliss that is to come as the reward of holiness is only attainable in eternity; and, as in Kant's ethical system, it is hopeless for a Christian to base his morality on the hope of happiness or the fear of God, for the Christian principle of morality does not make the knowledge of God and His Will the foundation of these laws, but only the foundation of the *summum bonum*, or the Kingdom of God, which can only be entered by a disinterestedly moral disposition, made possible by the freedom of the will. In other words, Christianity is an ethically valid religion—not obedience to a will that is imposed from without, and therefore " goodness " motivated by fear or hope of reward, but a consciousness in man that his will is in harmony with the will of God ; hence a belief in the goodness of God, and the idea that happiness in eternity will follow for those who have entered His Kingdom.

The Relation of the Postulates to the Three Ideas of Theoretic Reason

Thus, out of the moral law and the conception of the *summum bonum* which it commands us to strive towards, and which must therefore be regarded as ultimately realisable, we have three necessary postulates—the immortality of the soul, the freedom of the will, and the existence of God. These postulates are closely related to the three Ideas of theoretical reason considered in Part III. It was there described how reason in its theoretical use presented these ideas to itself as problems to be solved, but was unable to supply the solution. Thus (1) the attempt to demonstrate theoretically the permanence of the thinking subject only led to what Kant called a paralogism, involving as it did a confusion of the subject presupposed in all knowledge of objects, and only in that respect permanent, with an object known under the category of substance; (2) the attempt in cosmology to determine the world as a system complete in itself led to an antinomy, the only suggested solution of which was a distinction between the phenomenal and noumenal worlds, but which distinction theoretic reason had no means of proving; and (3) the Idea of the absolute being, or the theological conception of the first Being, was a mere ideal which reason was able to think but never to realise. Now, however, all three Ideas, which theoretic reason could not decide either for or against, are established as objective facts by the moral law. (1) The permanence of the soul becomes a necessary postulate because of the endless duration required for the realisation of the *summum bonum;* (2) the reality of a free noumenal world, as opposed to the world of phenomenal necessity, is forced on us by the idea of freedom involved in the conception of ourselves as responsible agents under the moral law; and (3) the Idea of God, or of a first Being, becomes verified by the necessity to postulate an independent Being uniting virtue and happiness for the realisation of the *summum bonum.* In other words, what theoretic reason had suggested and shown to be possible, but could never verify, practical reason establishes as real objects under the demands of the moral law.

Is our knowledge of the three Ideas extended in this way? it may be asked. Kant replies "Certainly, but only from the point of view of practice." Though we do not gain a knowledge of the nature of our souls, or of the intelligible world, or of the Supreme Being in the sense of knowing them as we know objects of cognition, we change the problematic conception of them into an assertion of their real existence, and have all the knowledge required for practical purposes. We cannot, it is true, bring any perception under these Ideas, so as to make any synthetic judgments concerning the objects, but in the sphere of practice they nevertheless become immanent and constitutive. " For they contain the grounds of the possibility of realising the necessary object of practical reason (the highest good), whereas theoretical reason finds in them merely regulative principles, which have their value in furthering the exercise of the intelligence in experience, but not in enabling us to gain any certitude as to the existence of any object beyond experience. When, however, by the moral consciousness we are put in possession of this new certitude, reason as a speculative faculty comes in (though properly only to protect its practical use), and goes to work with these Ideas in a negative way, i.e., not to extend but to elucidate them; and so to exclude, on the one hand, Anthropomorphism as the source of a superstition which pretends to enlarge our knowledge by a fictitious experience, and on the other hand, Fanaticism, which pretends to a similar enlargement of knowledge not by experience, but by means of supersensuous intuition or feeling. For both these equally are hindrances of the practical use of reason, and the exclusion of them may be regarded as an extension of our knowledge in a practical point of view.

" When these Ideas of God, of an intelligible world, and of immortality, are determined by predicates which are taken from our own nature, we must regard this determination neither as a sensualising of these pure Ideas (Anthropomorphism), nor as a transcendent knowledge of supersensible objects ; for the predicates we use are only understanding and will, and, indeed, these regarded only in that relation to each other in which we are required by the moral law to regard them. All other psychological characteristics of our understanding and will, which we empirically observe in the exercise of those faculties (as, e.g., that our understanding is discursive and not intuitive, that our ideas follow each other in time, that our will is dependent for its satisfaction on the existence of its object, etc.—all characteristics, in short, which cannot be attributed to the understanding and will of the Supreme Being) we necessarily leave out of account. There remains, therefore, of all the conceptions through which we think of a pure intelligence only those which are necessary to the possibility of a moral law : in other words, we have a knowledge of God solely from a practical point of view. If, on the other hand, we attempt to go beyond this, or to enlarge it to a theoretical knowledge of God, how must we think of Him ? We must attribute to Him an understanding which does not merely think but perceive, and a will which is directed to objects on the existence of which its satisfaction is not at all dependent, (not to mention such transcendental predicates as that His existence must have a quantity, i.e. a duration, which yet is not in time, though time is the sole means whereby we can represent existence as a quantity). Now, of these attributes we can form no conception which can give us real *knowledge* of the object, or enable us *theoretically* to explain the existence of supersensuous beings, but only such a conception as is sufficient for practical purposes."

We are thus obliged to limit ourselves to " the conception of a relation of understanding to will which the practical law determines a priori, and to which the same practical law secures objective reality " ; but this is sufficient to enable us to know God as an Author of the world possessed of the highest perfection. For to comply with the conception of the *summum bonum*, he must be *omniscient* in order to know my inmost mental state in all cases and at all times ; *omnipotent*, in order to allot to it fitting consequences ; also *omnipresent, eternal*, etc. In this way, through this moral theology we are led to a knowledge of God in the full sense of the term; whereas, even if we admit the first part of the Cosmological proof of the existence of God, permitting ourselves to ascend from the finite world to its first cause, we could never regard the cause as containing more than the effect, and this would be inadequate to constitute God as all-wise and all-good. Our knowledge of God, as of the other Ideas, arises out of the relation of understanding to will which the practical law determines a priori, since it is only out of the moral law in which this relationship consists that we have the necessary conception of the *summum bonum*, and with it the necessity for the three postulates to comply with it. We postulate God as being just what we require Him or will Him to be, in the same way that we postulate freedom and immortality, for it is only out of the nature of our will that the postulates become necessary. Therefore " the righteous man may say : I *will* that there should be a God ; I *will* that, though *in* this natural world, I should not be *of* it, but should also belong to a purely intelligible world; finally, I *will* that my duration should be endless. I insist upon this, and will not let this conviction be taken from me " ; for " in this instance alone my interest, because I *must* not relax anything of it, inevitably determines my judgment, without regarding sophistries, however unable I may be to answer them or to oppose them with others more plausible." According to Kant, this is the one case where the " I will that a certain thing shall be " is equivalent to the assertion " it is ", and on no account is it to be regarded as a mere subjective wish deluding me into the assumption of the existence of its object, as in the case of the day dream of the lover who convinces himself of the great beauty of his bride, which beauty in fact exists nowhere but in his head. " I entirely concur," says Kant when dealing with such a possibility, " in all cases where the feeling of want is due to mere inclination or natural desire. Such a want cannot postulate the existence of the object wanted even for him who feels it ; much less can it be the ground of a demand or postulate which is universal. In this case, however, we have *a want of Reason*, springing not from the *subjective* ground of our wishes, but from an *objective* motive of the will, which binds every rational being, and hence authorises him a priori to presuppose the existence in nature of the conditions necessary for its satisfaction."

Having examined Kant's ethical theory in all its aspects and traced it up to its final theological position, it is not, perhaps, an inappropriate conclusion to consider for a moment how wisely or otherwise man's cognitive faculties are adapted to what this philosophy presents as his ultimate destination. In other words, assuming the realisation of the *summum bonum* as the ultimate purpose of the universe, can the means man has of gaining a knowledge of this purpose, and more particularly the various postulates necessary for it, be regarded as adequate, or would not knowledge of a more emphatic and precise type have been better suited to the end in view? Kant deals with the matter towards the end of "The Critique of Practical Reason." At first sight, he says, we may be inclined to think that, assuming the endeavour after the *summum bonum* is the destiny of humanity, then nature has endowed us with very niggardly knowledge for grasping the purpose, since in most human procedure it is regarded as necessary to state definitely what is required of a person and what will be the consequences of his fulfilling or failing to fulfil the requirement in question. In the case of a real moral end, however, a brief consideration of the matter will show us how worthless such a procedure would be. For supposing we were endowed with a full and definite knowledge of God, and his law, and our immortality, is it not perfectly clear that, though we should do as commanded, there would be no more moral disposition behind our actions than there is in the case of the man who refrains from crime because of the fear of imprisonment or the hope of reward? God and eternity with their awful majesty would stand unceasingly before our eyes, and instead of our actions arising out of a moral disposition that could be regarded as free, they would simply be the determined result of fear and hope, and the moral worth of such actions, on which alone in the eyes of supreme wisdom the worth of the person and even of the world depends, would cease to exist. Our whole conduct would be simply a mechanistic pursuit of our ultimate happiness, and moral consciousness would be faced with the impossibility of maintaining the disinterestedness in which alone its value can consist. But, "when it is quite otherwise with us, when with all the effort of our reason we have only a very obscure and doubtful view into the future, when the Governor of the world allows us only to conjecture His existence and His majesty, not to behold them or prove them clearly; and, on the other hand, the moral law within us, without promising or threatening anything with certainty, demands of us disinterested respect; and only when this respect has become active and dominant, does it allow us by means of it a prospect into the world of the super-sensible, and then only with weak glances: all this being so, there is room for a true moral disposition, immediately devoted to the law, and a rational creature can become worthy of sharing in the *summum bonum* that corresponds to the worth of his person and not merely to his actions. Thus, what the study of nature and of man teaches us sufficiently elsewhere may well be true here also; that the unsearchable wisdom by which we exist is not less worthy of admiration in what it has denied than in what it has granted."

INDEX

Age of enlightenment, 7
"Analytic," general problem of, 69, 70; statement of Kant's method of dealing with ditto, 70, 71; the three divisions of, 77, 78, 83, 84
"Analytic of Principles," 123–160
Analytical and synthetical judgments distinguished, 34, 35
Anselm, of Canterbury, 229
"Anticipation of perception," 136, 137
Antinomies of pure reason, how they arise, 185, 186, 187, 189; Kant's proofs of the same, 189, 190, 191; human interests in favour of the theses of, 193, 194, 195; ditto in favour of the antitheses of, 195, 196; general solution of, 196, 197, 198, 199; ditto more completely expressed, 199, 200, 201
Aristotle, 1, 92, 93
"Axiom of intuition," 135, 136

Bacon, 151
Berkeley, 157

Caird, E., 131, 141, 143, 144, 261, 262
Categories, general purport of the metaphysical deduction of, 84, 85, 86, 87, 88, 89; the logical judgments on which based, 89, 90, 91; complete list of, 91; Kant's division and explanation of, 91, 92, 93; general object of transcendental deduction of, 94, 95; general statement of what Kant seeks to prove in latter, 96, 97, 98, 99; summary of results of ditto, 121, 122
Categorical imperative, 266; the theorems by which Kant arrives at, 267, 268, 269; absolute nature of, 269, 270; the first formula of, as criterion of moral worth of acts in life, 270, 271, 272; second formula of, 272, 273, 274; third formula of, 274, 275
Causal Antinomy, solution of, 204, 205, 206, 207
Causality, principle of, Hume's theory of, 18, 19, 139, 140; Kant's answer to same, 138, 139, 140, 141, 143, 144
Continuity of the species, law of, 239, 240
Cosmological Ideas, general statement of how they arise, 180, 181, 182; more complete ditto, 182, 183; as distinguished from Rational Cosmology, 184; as regulative principles, 202, 203
"Critique of Pure Reason," general statement of its teachings, 23, 24; its three main problems, 27; the grand problem of, 39, 40, 41;

297

advantages of ditto, 44, 45; the science with which concerned, 42; "Refutation of Idealism" in, 157; its relation to the "Critique of Practical Reason," 249
"Critique of Practical Reason. *See* Kant's Ethical system
"Criticism," in the Kantean sense, 28

Descartes, 13, 151, 157, 229, 230
"Dialectic," general problem of, 160, 161, 162, 163; the three branches of and how they arise, 169, 170, 171, 172; Kant's theory of the nature of reason in, 162, 163, 164, 165; Kant's treatment of rational psychology in, 173, 174, 175, 176, 177, 178; ditto rational cosmology, 174–211; ditto rational theology, 212–235; the Ideas as regulative principles in, 236–247
Dogmatism, in the Kantean sense, 28, 42
Duty, idea of, as criterion of moral worth, 264, 265

Empirical ego, 105; as distinguished from transcendental ego, 255, 256, 259
Empiricist theory of Knowledge and its inadequacy, 9, 10, 11; Kant's final position in relation to, 149, 150, 151, 152

Fischer, Kuno, 89, 168
Fitche, 6
Freedom of the will, solution often causal antinomy applied to the problem, 208, 209, 210, 211; the negative treatment of this problem in "The Critique of Pure Reason," 249, 250, 251, 252, 253, 254, 255; positive treatment in "The Critique of Practical Reason," 255, 256, 257, 258, 259, 260

Galileo, 13, 14, 21
God, the existence of a necessary postulate of moral reason, 281, 282, 283, 284, 285; His purpose in creating the world, 286; how we may think of, 290, 291, 292, 293, 294. *See also* Idea of God
Good will, as criterion of moral worth, 262, 263; what constitutes ditto, 263

Hedonism, Kant's moral system as an answer to, 261, 262
Hegel, 6
Herbart, 6
Hobbes, 21
Homogeneity, law of, 238
Hume, David, his scepticism, 8, 16; its effect on Kant, 17, 18; his empiricism, 9, 16, 17; his theory of causality, 18, 19, 139, 140; Kant's answer to the same, 138, 139, 140, 141, 143, 144; Kant's position in relation to, 148, 149, 150, 151, 152

Idea of God, how it arises, 213, 214, 215, 216; as distinguished from rational theology, 216; natural manner in which the mind attempts to establish the existence of an object corresponding to, 217, 218; assumptions involved in same, 219, 220; summary of the three proofs by which it is attempted to establish the objective reality of, 220, 221; the teleological proof and its refutation, 221, 222, 223, 224, 225; ditto the Cosmological, 225, 226, 227, 228, 229; ditto the Ontological, 229, 230, 231, 232, 233, 234; the objective reality of, necessitated by the moral law, 279, 280, 281, 282, 283, 284, 285, 286, 287, 289, 290; is knowledge of God extended thereby, 290, 291, 292, 293, 294

Ideas of pure reason, general nature of, 160, 161, 162, 163; different forms of, 169, 170, 171, 172; the problem they present, 170, 171, 172; their immanent use as regulative principles, 136, 137, 241, 242, 243, 244, 245, 246

Kant, his generally recognised status in philosophy, 1; his early education and later life, 2, 3; his general achievements in philosophy, 4, 5, 6; his central position in metaphysics, 6; his early training and the subsequent influence of Hume, 15, 16, 17, 18, 19, 20; his position in relation to Rationalism and Empiricism, 23, 24, 25, 149, 150, 151, 152; his problem as set out in the Prolegomena, 27; his answer to Hume's scepticism, 138, 139, 140, 141, 143, 144; his treatment of the Idea of God (*see* Rational Theology, and Moral Theology); his moral theology as compared with Christianity, 287, 288

Kepler, 14

Kingdom of ends, Kant's conception of, 275, 276

Leibniz, 15, 102, 149, 150, 151, 152, 153, 229, 230, 231

Locke, 22, 29, 151

Lotze, 6

Mathematics, nature of the judgments of, 36, 37; a priori space and time perception as basis of, 57, 58, 59, 60, 61, 62; metaphysical principles of, 135, 136, 137, 138

Metaphysics, how possible as a natural disposition of the mind, 40, 41, 160, 161, 162, 163

"Metaphysic of Ethics," the good as defined in, 262, 263, 264, 265, 269

Metaphysical Deduction of the Categories, the purpose and contention of same, 84, 85, 86, 87, 88, 89; the logical judgments on which the categories are based, 89, 90, 91; complete list of categories, 91; Kant's division and explanation of the same, 92, 93

Metaphysical principles of science, Kant's general division of, 129, 130, 131; general distinction between the mathematical and dynamical principles of, 131, 132, 133, 134, 135; the mathematical principles of, 135, 136, 137, 138; dynamical principles of, 138, 139, 140, 141, 142, 143, 144, 145, 146, 147

Moral feeling, 276, 277

Moral freedom. *See* Freedom of the Will

Moral law, formulation of, 261, 262, 263, 264, 265, 266, 267, 268, 269, 270; application of, 270, 271, 272, 273, 274, 275, 276, 277, 278; first formula of, 270, 271, 272; second formula of, 272, 273, 274; third formula of, 274, 275

Moral theology, Kant's, 279, 280, 281, 282, 283, 284, 285, 286, 287, 288, 289, 290, 291, 292, 293, 294, 295, 296

Necessity and universality, as the means of distinguishing pure and empirical knowledge, 31, 32, 33

Newton, 13, 14, 21

Noumena and phenomena, division of the world into, 152, 153, 154, 155, 156, 157, 158, 159; noumena in the positive and negative sense, 154; justifiable nature of the latter, 155, 156; criticism of Kant's position in relation to, 157, 158

Paralogisms, of rational psychology, 175, 176, 177

"Postulates of Empirical Thought," 145, 146, 147

Postulates of moral reason, their relation to the Ideas of pure reason, 288, 289, 290; is knowledge of the latter extended thereby, 290, 291, 292, 293, 294

Practical reason, what Kant means by, 249, 250, 251

"Preestablished harmony," Leibniz's, 116, 117

Principle of causality, 138, 139, 140, 141, 142, 143, 144

Principle of reciprocity, 138, 139, 140, 141, 142, 143, 144, 145

Principle of the permanence of substance, 138, 139, 140, 141, 142, 143

Principles of the pure understanding, 129-149

Productive imagination, 119, 124, 125

Rational Cosmology, general problem of, 179, 180; as distinguished from the Cosmological Idea, 181, 182

Rational psychology, general fallacy of, 173, 174, 175; the four contentions of, 175, 176; Kant's answer to these, 176, 177; Kant's general conclusion in relation to, 177, 178

Rational theology, general statement of Kant's treatment of the problem of, 212, 213; combination of the two conceptions it seeks to establish, 217; summary of the three proofs by which it endeavours to show the existence of God, 220, 221; the Teleological proof and its refutation, 221, 222, 223, 224, 225; ditto the Cosmological, 225, 226, 227, 228, 229; ditto the Ontological, 229, 230, 231, 232, 233, 234; Kant's general conclusions in relation to, 234, 235

Rationalist theory of knowledge, 10, 11; its inadequacy, 12, 13; Kant's final position in relation to, 149, 150, 151, 152

Reason, Kant's theory of the nature of, 162, 163; syllogisms of, 163, 164, 165; examples of the three different forms of latter, 165

Regulative principles, the Ideas as, 136, 137, 241, 242, 243, 244, 245, 246

Reproductive imagination, 119

Robertson, Prof. C., 71

INDEX 301

Scepticism, in Kantian sense, 28; Hume's, 8, 16; Kant's position in relation to, 148, 149, 150, 151, 152

Science, its progress in 17th and 18th centuries and the effect of this on philosophy, 13, 14; synthetical judgments a priori as basic principles of, 36, 37, 38, 39; the metaphysical principles of, 127-147

Schelling, 6

Schopenhauer, 5

Self, object self and subject self distinguished, 255, 256, 259

Schemata of the categories of quantity, 126; Ditto quality, 126, 127; Ditto relation, 127, 128; Ditto, modality, 128

Schematism of the categories, 123-129

Sense and understanding, their relation, 46, 47, 72, 73, 74, 75; the union of, 115, 116, 117, 118, 119, 120

Sensuous propensity, man's versus the law of reason, 258, 259, 266, 267, 268

Soul, the Idea of, 170; contentions of rational psychology in relation to, 173, 174, 175, 176; Kant's answer to same, 176, 177; the unknowable nature of the, 177, 178; immortality of a necessary postulate of moral reason, 279, 280, 281

Space and time, general statement of Kant's doctrine of, 49, 50; Kant's proofs that they are a priori representations, 51, 52, 53, 54; what kind of a priori representations (percepts or concepts), 54, 55, 56, 57; transcendental exposition of, 57, 58, 59, 60, 61, 62; Kant's conclusions as to the nature of, 62, 63, 64, 65; space and time as distinguished from such subjective determinations as colour, taste, etc., to which no ideality attaches, 65, 66

Specification, law of, 238, 239

Spinoza, 151

Summum bonum, the problems it raises, 279, 280; why it demands the immortality of the soul, 281; ditto the existence of God, 281, 282, 283, 284, 285

Syllogisms of reason, different forms of, 163, 164, 165; true and false syllogisms, 167, 168, 169, 171

Synthetical judgments a priori, 35, 36; ditto as the basis of mathematics, 36, 37; ditto as the basis of pure physics, 38, 39

" Synthesis intellectualis," 118

" Synthesis speciosa," 118

Torricelli, 13

Transcendental Æsthetic, the problem of the Æsthetic, 48; distinction of " matter " and " form " in, 48; general statement of Kant's treatment of space and time in, 49, 50; Kant's conclusions in, 62, 63, 64, 65. *See also* Space and Time

" Transcendental Deduction of the Categories," general object of, 94, 95; statement of what Kant seeks to prove in, 96, 97, 98, 99; summary of results of, 121, 122

Transcendental ego, 105; as distinguished from empirical ego, 255, 256, 259

Transcendental logic, as compared with general logic, 75, 76, 77; the three divisions of, 77, 78, 79

Transcendental synthesis of the imagination, 118, 119
Transcendental unity of apperception, 100, 101, 102, 103, 104, 105, 106, 107 ; as distinguished from empirical apperception, 107, 108, 109 ; the categories as the means of bringing the manifold of sense under, 109, 110, 111, 112, 113, 114

Transcendentalism, defined, 41

Universe, Idea of. *See* Cosmology

Wolff's metaphysic, 15
Wolff-Liebniz philosophy, Kant's position in relation to, 149, 150, 151, 152

For Product Safety Concerns and Information please contact our EU representative GPSR@taylorandfrancis.com
Taylor & Francis Verlag GmbH, Kaufingerstraße 24, 80331 München, Germany

www.ingramcontent.com/pod-product-compliance
Lightning Source LLC
Chambersburg PA
CBHW071803300426
44116CB00009B/1186